Calling the Shots
THE CAPTAIN'S STORY

Calling the Shots
THE CAPTAIN'S STORY

MICHAEL VAUGHAN

with Martin Hardy

HODDER &
STOUGHTON

First published in Great Britain in 2005 by Hodder & Stoughton
A division of Hodder Headline

A Hodder paperback

1

A CIP catalogue record for this title is available from the British Library

ISBN 978 0 340 89630 2
ISBN 0 340 89630 2

Typeset in Sabon by
Rowland Phototypesetting Ltd,
Bury St Edmunds, Suffolk

Printed in Great Britain by
Clays Ltd, St Ives plc

Hodder Headline's policy is to use papers that are natural,
renewable and recyclable products and made from wood grown
in sustainable forests. The logging and manufacturing processes are expected
to conform to the environmental regulations of the country of origin.

Hodder & Stoughton Ltd
A division of Hodder Headline
338 Euston Road
London NW1 3BH

*Connor Shaw, a young boy whose
bravery has been an inspiration
to all who have met him.*

CONTENTS

ACKNOWLEDGEMENTS

All the people – family, friends and colleagues – who have helped me in one way or another with this book are too many to mention. They know who they are and I say a big thank you to them.

In particular, I must mention my wife Nichola for not only giving me her love, friendship and our daughter Tallulah Grace, but also for her never-ending support when I have needed it most. The England cricket captain has not always been the easiest to live with but Nichola has never complained and keeps me in touch with reality.

My job as captain would be impossible without the assistance and backing of all the players, coaching staff, cricket board and backroom staff. Everybody connected with Team England, not least sponsors Vodafone, have played a huge part in what we have achieved over the last few years.

The team at International Sports Management, headed by Chubby Chandler and assisted by his cricket director Neil Fairbrother, the former England player, has ensured that I have been able to concentrate totally on the captaincy without worry about my off-field interests.

I am also indebted to the team at Hodder & Stoughton

for giving me the chance to share my two years of captaincy, especially my indefatigable editor Roddy Bloomfield, whose enthusiasm for this project has known no bounds.

Finally, my thanks to sports writer and author Martin Hardy, who said he would never write another book after the last and now can't wait for the next.

PHOTOGRAPHIC ACKNOWLEDGEMENTS

The author and publisher would like to thank the following for permission to reproduce photographs:

Philip Brown, Winston Bynorth, Colorsport, Getty Images, PA/Empics, Reuters.

PREFACE

It was only in South Africa, towards the end of our ill-fated World Cup mission of 2003, that I first seriously started thinking about the prospect of leading England. I had previously, albeit briefly, fantasised about what it might feel like being first down the steps at Lord's, Delhi or Sydney and as the rumours surrounding Nasser Hussain's future as captain intensified, so did my interest in being his successor.

While our future in the World Cup and the fiasco about whether it was safe, or morally right, for us to play in Zimbabwe remained unresolved, I refused to give the captaincy a great deal of thought. I got on with my own job and stuck to the belief, as all fatalists do, that things eventually end up with those who deserve them. What will be, will be. But as our future was determined, my mind wandered more and more towards what would happen now. Michael Vaughan, captain of England. The more I thought about it, the more I was sure I wanted the job. I felt I was up to the task, and I was enthused by the prospect of making an impression on the game we gave to the world, maybe even leaving a rich legacy through which England would again become cricket's dominant force. I knew I would feel comfortable calling the shots, but there was another driving force: I wanted to lead a team capable of winning the Ashes.

There had been rumours throughout the World Cup that Nasser was going to quit as captain at the end of it: definitely in one-dayers and possibly even at Test level. Indeed, he had indicated himself that he was likely to give it all up in one go, although the press speculated that there would be an overlap – a new one-day captain while Nasser continued to lead the Test side.

Many names got bandied around as possible successors and I knew that all those mentioned were capable of doing a good job. Adam Hollioake, a one-day specialist, Marcus Trescothick, considered Nasser's deputy, the vastly experienced Mark Butcher, Kent's captain David Fulton and myself were all mentioned. There were plenty of candidates and it would have been easy to make a case for any of them.

The conjecture grew after Zimbabwe's crucial game against Pakistan in Bulawayo was washed out. That result meant we were on our way home, our interest in the World Cup coming to a soggy end in circumstances totally out of our control. Nasser, Ashley Giles, Paul Collingwood and myself were playing golf at the time, but kept in touch with matters in Bulawayo through telephone calls. I could tell from Nasser's demeanour on the course, where he is extremely competitive and normally locked in to the matters in hand, that his mind was elsewhere. Ash and I were thrashing him and Colly, but that's not what he was worried about, no matter the blow to his pocket. Nasser's thoughts were fully explained shortly after we finished playing. Within a couple of hours, a meeting was called and he announced his resignation as one-day captain, while remaining in charge of the Test side.

The coach Duncan Fletcher said a few words on behalf of the players, thanking him for his efforts, Nasser did a press conference and then we flew home, leaving South Africa, Zimbabwe and a troubled winter behind us.

I'd just had the best winter of my career with the bat, with three centuries in an Ashes series in Australia. So there was a lot of local interest when I arrived home in Sheffield – where to this day I retain the same circle of friends I have enjoyed since before anybody knew me as a cricketer. Invariably, the question of the captaincy would crop up, and when asked, be it by friends, colleagues, journalists or England's management, my only reply was that I would like to be considered. I never did an interview saying I wanted the job, but I did offer the thought that if my name was mentioned then I would consider it an honour. I kept my mouth shut and hoped that the selection panel would see something in me that warranted the offer of the job. I had made it clear during an early phone call from the chairman of selectors David Graveney that I was keen and now it was up to them to decide.

I'd never captained Yorkshire although I had led the England A team. Obviously, I didn't have much experience. But all I wanted was for them to see something in me rather than my having to persuade them that I was the right man. That's the way I have always looked at any position. I wanted them to want me. I felt I could help bring success to the national team.

I had enjoyed a great year so my confidence was high. I felt we had a side who were good players and good lads. We had an excellent coach and management team so it was a good position to go into. Not many changes were needed. I'd captained quite a lot of the players before on the A tour:

Andrew Flintoff, Steve Harmison, Robert Key and Vikram Solanki. I wanted to test myself even though I knew it would be a tough job; I wanted the challenge; I wanted no regrets later in life or daydreams about what might have been . . . if only. I also spoke to friends and family, Neil Fairbrother, formerly of Lancashire and England and now director of cricket with my management company International Sports Management, Chubby Chandler, ISM's chief executive, and a few of the players. They all said that it was an opportunity I would have to take if offered.

Finally, in early May, the announcement came. I remember going to Hillside Golf Club in Lancashire with Chubby and Fairbrother, the European Tour golfers David Howell and Mark Foster, and David O'Leary, soon to be appointed Aston Villa manager and a man I would later consult about player-management skills. We were to play a round and then go on to football's Old Trafford to watch Manchester United in the Champions League.

I was on the patio waiting to tee off when my mobile phone rang and the screen announced that it was Duncan Fletcher. I remember him asking what I thought I would bring to the job, but my cards remained close to my chest. Again I just said that it was up to others to determine whether they thought I had the necessary qualities. I did want the job but I placed the onus firmly on them. Some would interpret that as a high-risk strategy and would have gone shouting that they wanted the job, but that's one thing I don't do.

Our golf party moved on to Old Trafford and as we entered the Theatre Of Dreams the selection panel was deciding whether I was about to realise one of mine. The following morning would reveal the answer. Graveney's question was short and simple: 'Do you want the job?' I thought for a second before giving a shorter and simpler reply: 'Yes.' I don't remember any of the conversation after that or even if I heard anything else. A new era of English one-day cricket was about to start, with me calling the shots.

The good luck messages flooded in and, as ever, it was nice to hear from David English, who does great work for schools' cricket and charity and heads the Bunbury cricket team, extracting the urine in his inimitable fashion: 'Hello Vaughny, it's the loon here . . .' Many people seemed genuinely delighted and I was determined not to let them down – although it would only be later that I fully realised what I had taken on.

For the two years leading up to Nasser's abdication, Marcus had looked like the player who was going to take over. He had been the unofficial vice-captain and took over whenever Nasser was not on the field. A lot of people thought it was a natural progression and Trescothick had publicly said that he would welcome the opportunity to lead his country. But as soon as I got the job, he was the first to call and say, 'Well done.' He's not the kind of person who holds grudges or says: 'I'm not going to play with you.' He wished me all the best and said he was looking forward to playing under my captaincy. Ask anybody who's captained him and they'd all say the same, you can't wish for a better person in your team. You know what you are getting – a world-class player and a world-class team man.

Meanwhile, the Surrey captain Hollioake had said that he thought he was past it and the job should go to me. It was what you'd expect from Adam because he's never been one to push himself forward. I don't think he really cared whether it went to me or Trescothick, as long as it went to somebody who would be in the team for the next few years.

There was always going to be the issue of the captaincy and my batting, whether or not the extra responsibility would affect my form. In one sense it was not such a big question because I didn't have a lot of form to lose: I had not exactly sent the scoreboard into overdrive in the one-day arena. I just wanted the opportunity to take a new team forward. It was my chance to make a mark on the English one-day game.

1

FIRST AMONG EQUALS:
The One-Day Captaincy

Sometimes the captaincy can get talked up too much, its importance magnified way too far. If you win you're the best thing since Hovis first put a slicer through one of its loaves; if you lose, you're just another piece of burnt toast. There is no middle ground. You get either too much praise or excessive criticism. It can never be as black and white as that although I think captaincy today is more difficult than it has ever been. There is more spotlight on the leader and he comes under intense and consistent scrutiny simply because there have never been as many cameras – covering every angle of the ground and its surrounds – as there are nowadays.

Wherever the captain is there will be a camera trained on him, watching his mannerisms, trying to detect any weaknesses, reading his body language. It's almost as if they are trying to invade your soul. If they could put a camera in the loo they would and I wouldn't put it past Sky to ask for one.

Nothing can detract, however, from knowing that you get to lead out your country at places like Lord's. There is a massive buzz in being captain although it is not in evidence quite so much when you are trying to sort out whether nets should be at 1.30pm or 2.

I would quickly realise that being captain makes you a lot better known and recognisable. Before, when I'd played well I could still sneak around and not get recognised too often, but all that changed. When you're just a player you don't realise what comes with being captain.

Before the 2003 home season started, I had to travel down to Lord's to give my first press conference. I spoke to the media and gave the spiel that all new captains come out with. I had my picture taken a million times: the first words spoken by cameramen the world over were probably not 'm-m-mum' or 'd-d-dad', but 'Just one more'.

I realised what I had taken on when I saw the number of people who turned up, and it sank in completely when they took me indoors and parked me in front of the wall where all the photographs of my predecessors hang. I knew what I was getting into, or at least I thought I did. But I was deter-mined to try it, and not to let it become a millstone. I knew the one-day team was going to take a new shape because we wanted to build towards the next World Cup in 2007. The likes of Nasser, Andy Caddick, Nick Knight, Craig White and Alec Stewart – all players who had been in the squad of 2003 – would be missing next time round. None was actually dropped, they all retired from the international one-day scene. It made for an exciting time because I was a new captain and I would have new, young and enthusiastic players. Now I had to help choose them.

Being one-day captain did not excuse me from county duty and immediately after the media session I had to get a lift from an ECB official to March, where Yorkshire were play-ing Cambridgeshire in the qualifying stages of the C&G Trophy. The journalists just followed and soon there they were watching the new England captain play Cambridge-shire.

At that match I was just one of the lads in the Yorkshire dressing room. I got plenty of stick, good-natured banter, nothing I hadn't encountered a thousand times before, but this time it was slightly different. Mixed with the irreverence was a certain respect and pride that one of the Yorkshire lads was now England one-day captain.

But before I took charge for the first time, there was still the question of Test duty under Nasser. For me, that was no problem at all. I didn't feel any different although the atmosphere in the Test dressing room would soon change after I had led the one-day team.

We played two Tests against Zimbabwe, won them both, but I didn't trouble the scorers too often. Afterwards I returned to Yorkshire for a few games and then England met up in Cardiff to prepare for three one-day matches against the Pakistanis in the NatWest Challenge, which would be followed by a triangular involving Zimbabwe and South Africa.

We picked a lot of players with little one-day international experience and at the first team meeting in the Marriott Hotel, Cardiff, I introduced three themes that would recur: fitness, enjoyment and personal responsibility.

I'd looked at the England team and seen just how many matches had been missed by some key players, myself included, because of injuries. This was not a common, global failure. Looking around the world, most of the other teams' key players seemed to be playing more of the important matches. Andrew Flintoff, Steve Harmison, myself: we had all missed far too many games. It was a situation that had to be addressed.

We sat down in Cardiff and I told them that whatever our trainer, Nigel Stockill, asked us to do, we'd do it. He would not demand anything that would be detrimental to our game or body; he would be doing it because he felt it would make us stronger, fitter and more athletic. All the fitness preparation was passed on to him. Whatever he says, we do, I stressed again. For me, that included bulking up, and I deliberately put on an extra stone. I realise the importance of fitness, but I must admit I enjoy training much more afterwards than during.

I asked the players to use Fletcher as much as they wanted, if they hadn't done already, to work on technique and tactics because I felt he had much to offer in those areas. I invited them to go looking for him once they knew they had a problem or concern rather than waiting for him to come to them.

But the one thing I stressed more than anything was enjoyment. I said: 'Listen, we used to enjoy everything when we were playing for Yorkshire, Kent, Middlesex or wherever when we were schoolboys. Just because it is international cricket – with more pressure, spectators and media attention – it is still the same game. We should try to play it whenever possible with a smile and a feeling of joy.' There are stages when cricket is difficult to enjoy, but when I am going through a dodgy patch I just keep returning to my philosophy – don't take yourself or the game too seriously. You have to think and analyse sometimes, but if you are doing it all the time and not enjoying it then you'd go absolutely bonkers and become very weary very quickly.

I told the players to look after their own discipline and tried to put the emphasis on them doing things themselves rather than my having to shout at them. I told them that as international cricketers they should know exactly what they had to do and exactly what was required for them to get the best out of themselves. They should not need myself, Duncan or Nigel Stockill to say you have to go to bed at eight, nine or 10 or 12, you shouldn't drink a glass of wine or have a few beers. You should know yourself what you have to do to get yourself right for the next game of cricket. I just asked them to try to work out their own gameplan both on and off the pitch.

It's very hard for others to tell them what to do because those others are not inside a player's head. It's the same when you make a mistake, it's only you who knows the real reason why you made it. A coach can give you a few tips and assume a few things, but it's only you who knows what's going on inside.

I also asked the players to manage their own space. In practice, you know what you need to work on, and you should not go hiding from that – don't just work at things you are good at, but confront the things that you aren't as good at. Only you know deep down your deficiencies, nobody else does. That sort of honesty takes trust – in the management and selectors – and I was determined to keep building that. Preparation would be another key. If I saw a player doing nothing in preparation, but performing in a match situation then I had not the slightest problem. But I get upset if a player doesn't know how to prepare properly by the time he has reached international level. It's different if you are 20 or 21 because it takes time to get to know your own game, body and strategies. If we prepared correctly and also analysed the opposition carefully, performance would look after itself. If you prepare right and perform badly that's one of those things, but if you don't prepare properly, haven't given yourself the best chance, then there are no excuses. I kept telling the players to work out what they had to do to get the most out of themselves. We would help if asked but not dictate.

We also tried to identify exactly what role every player has in the team. Myself and Duncan sat down with every player to address this. If you don't know your specific role it can be very difficult and you can end up playing in a way which isn't good for the overall picture or the team. If you do know it, then it makes our job easier because once you have given a guy a role or job he knows what to work on in practice. Even with fielding positions, we try to find areas where every player will field – Trescothick at slip or sweeping on the boundary; Collingwood always at backward point. We did it so that every player knew exactly what to work on. Another example was Darren Gough, who would have the new ball and come back to bowl his yorkers at the end. So he knew which areas of the game he would have to perform in.

We didn't just give the player a role, we asked everyone to tell us what they had in mind. We had our own ideas, but we wanted it to come from the players themselves. About 90% of the time, they said exactly what we had written down. With the two or three who weren't as sure, we discussed and debated it and eventually they left the room with a job both they and we were happy with.

The exercise also helped us learn how a player was thinking. It can be daunting for a youngster sitting in a room with the captain and coach and maybe one or two of the senior guys, but it's amazing how much you can learn about somebody from the way they listen and talk. We tried to say very little and get them to say a lot. That way you very quickly understand a player's cricket brain – and in some ways gauge his ability.

We had a lot of applicants wanting to bat between No. 1 and No. 4 but we had to get everybody to understand that they might have to go between No. 5 and No. 7. In one-day cricket that's the hardest place to bat. The situation changes fast and you have to have a very, very good cricket brain, assessing any and every situation quickly. There are times when you have to rebuild a bad start and other times when you have to accelerate from ball one. We saw in a few players the ability to do that, Paul Collingwood being the best example.

Before Pakistan, we played Glamorgan (in the guise of Wales), who are a very good one-day team. The opposition didn't matter, it was essential for me to see us win and watch the way we went about it. I was heartened by what I saw. We went out that night as a squad and had a few drinks to relax and celebrate. I thought it important that we went out together as much as we could; that way, even though you will always have the friends you are closer to than others, you don't get cliques. Previously, we had been going out in separate groups and separate cars, but now I wanted us to be a unit both on and off the pitch.

We then travelled to Manchester United's training ground for a session on the Sunday, fixed up by our shared sponsor, Vodafone. It was a bit claustrophobic on the coach, but it was good to have the whole squad together and the banter was flying. The camaraderie in general was very good and travelling together, rather than separately as some previous England sides had, helped develop team spirit.

Steve Bull, our sports psychologist, conducted a few sessions and we had a kick around followed by an exercise which included wooden building blocks. If you expressed incredulity at that last statement, it was nothing compared to what some of the players thought. We were arranged into three teams and putting the wooden blocks together correctly took a lot of preparation, planning and communication – and a lot of time plotting the decisions to be taken. You could see many of the players thinking: 'What the hell has this got to do with cricket?', but actually there were a lot of parallels. There was plenty of planning, which you need for any sport, you had to communicate with your team-mates and you had to make the right decision at the right time, another essential in a winning team.

Each of the six players in a group had to collect three pieces of wood, and the team had to put these things down in specific order. If you missed your turn the whole project collapsed. You had to have a good strategy in place. It was a good lesson for myself and Duncan to see which players were the smart ones. The ones who were clever in the exercise were also the ones who were playing clever cricket. It told us quite a lot.

The following day brought my first full international match in charge. Manchester is my birthplace and endless numbers of family and friends wanted to come to the game. We had a team talk the night before and, as usual, we went through the opposition player by player. Duncan said a few words and then it was over to the video analyst Malcolm Ashton to examine the strengths and weaknesses of the opposition. After Malcolm's video show, the meeting was thrown open and anybody who had anything to say was encouraged to do so. We talked about one or two big issues, in particular their spinners and main strike threat Shoaib Akhtar, before Fletch went through everything again quickly.

The floor was then mine and I emphasised that we were a young team: we should not put too much pressure on ourselves. That came with the territory anyway so there was no need to add to it. I encouraged them to enjoy the day, express themselves and to use their enthusiasm to drive us on. I also wanted our fielding to be electric. I went through our starting XI believing it important that the XI on duty should know the night before because it can be difficult if you don't. In fact, I try to tell them as early as possible, but that is not always easy because of the weather, injuries or the state of the wicket. That was not the case here and as we went to dinner and then our rooms I was sure we were all ready for what was ahead.

I remember being very nervous that first morning, just as nervous, if not more so, as when I made my Yorkshire and England debuts. My phone never stopped until I turned it off. It was time for the short journey to Old Trafford in what we call our No. 2s, which to the rest of the world means smart casual.

You could tell there was going to be a big crowd and that Pakistan would have huge support. Hooters and klaxons were already piercing the air. The thing about day/night matches is that the toss is terribly important, giving the side who bat first a huge advantage. On this occasion, we were of the opinion that it would be crucial. I remember walking out with an amazing sense of pride that I was England captain. It was a wonderful feeling. The coin went up and came down on our side. One toss, one win – great record, although it's gone a bit downhill since. We didn't get a bad start – 152 for four in the 32nd over – and I remember the wicket being pretty good, smashing a six and then there being a mini-collapse. We finished up getting 204, which wasn't great, and Pakistan came out fighting – they have every shot and every trick in the book and some very experienced players. I wasn't sure if we had enough runs.

One of the things I had introduced was the huddle on the pitch. Leicestershire had been doing it at county level for a few seasons and I'd seen it in football and rugby matches. I felt it gave the team a good sense of togetherness when first going out on to the pitch. It's not so much what's said, but the feeling of being together. But I did say on that day that playing against Pakistan you are never out of the game because the unexpected can always happen and often does. I just said let's enjoy the fielding and the atmosphere and have a go. If we do that and still lose then we can't complain.

We did lose, but it was a close-run thing. Jimmy Anderson and Goughy did well at the end and Rikki Clarke produced an impressive spell on his debut. It was a decent performance from a young set of players on a night when it would have been easy to be overawed. I was pleased and proud at the way we fought back, although I could have done without the pitch invasion after they'd won. It was about 10.30pm and we were all knackered when we found ourselves having to sprint off to avoid being crushed by about 1,000 fans. It's quite scary when they all start running at you. You basically have to put your head down and get off as fast as you can.

As I went to bed, I reflected on the fact that already – after just one game in charge – some things in the team had changed. The huddle for example. I'd decided it was something we would do, but that it would not necessarily be me who spoke all the time. I wanted to try to give other players opportunity to see what it was like to be the captain. I'd tell whoever was to speak the night before so they had time to think about it. Sometimes you could talk about absolute crap and we'd just have a bit of a giggle, but on other occasions there would be something more serious to get over.

I'd said when I took over that I wanted 11 captains on the pitch and a lot was made of it. I think people thought I was passing the buck, trying to get others to do the work, but I firmly believe when you are out in the field you should be thinking like a captain, thinking of the next bowling or fielding change. As a leader, it's great when people come up with ideas because it is very easy to miss things. No matter how young or old a player was, how vast or tiny their experience, if they had an idea I wanted them to tell me. Then I'd decide what to do, whether to act on it or ignore it. This wasn't confined to the pitch either. Anything that involved the team – training, preparation, behaviour, standards – absolutely anything, then their input would be appreciated if not necessarily implemented. I'd take it on board if it was good and say thanks, but no thanks if it was not.

I hope it helped the players feel that they could get involved more. There are captains, and Nasser was one, who like to do everything on their own. That's the way he did the job. He wanted to make every decision and I'm not saying that's wrong, just that it wasn't the way I wanted to do it. I wanted to be a leader who could get the best out of others by delegation. I wanted other people to be making decisions, that way they would be involved all the time and there was less chance of their mind wandering and a mistake being made.

And if people start thinking, isn't this the Australian philosophy, then all I'll say is that whether we like the Aussies or not, they run a great cricket team. I'm not too proud to say that their system is one I would embrace and copy. I'd also duplicate the way they train. I have tried to get as much of an insight into the way they do things as I can. These ideas were just a reflection of my natural instincts. I have never read a book on captaincy and although I had respect for those I had served under – David Byas, Martyn Moxon and Darren Lehmann at Yorkshire; Stewart and Hussain with England – it was only in Nasser's last couple of years that I started really thinking about leadership. Even when I led the England A tour I didn't really think much about it. I just tried to do it in a way I liked. I admired Australia's Steve Waugh. People say it's difficult to judge him as a captain because he had a great team. I always say in response that he may have had a great team, but he also had to drive them on to win every game because people expected victory. He must have had superb man-management skills and personal motivation to keep that drive in their side. You need great players to win consistently, but you also have to know how to treat them. They can sometimes be the hardest to manage. He had ten other great players: for them to keep listening to his ideas and what he had to say, he must have had a lot of respect.

When Nasser was captain he did everything himself and I didn't really feel as if I had much of an input. If I had an opinion I thought it might not be welcomed. That made me wander a bit on the pitch because I didn't feel that I was going in the same direction as the captain. Maybe I wasn't confident enough in my own ability or wasn't secure enough of my position in the team to think that Nasser would want to hear my advice. He may not believe in my methods now but all I am trying to do is make it as open and as honest as I can for everybody.

I have always thought that if you're a bowler, then you want your own field. The bowler is the only one who knows where he's aiming and that gives him the best idea where the fielders should be. He also knows in his own mind how he is bowling and whether he wants a more attacking or defensive field. That's why I try to tell them to be honest. If they are feeling a bit ropey and I've put four slips and a gully in and they don't necessarily want that field, then they have to be honest and tell me. There can be a lot of bravado and front in cricket and it often obscures someone's real feelings and leads to problems. If I feel that I have to overrule the bowler for the sake of the match and the team, then I do. But I can't think of anything worse than knowing you are bowling to the wrong field. It's like me batting and somebody saying: You're going to take guard on off stump today. I'd say naff off. I'll bat where I want to bat, I'll play the way I want to play. That's also how I'd look on it if I was a bowler. People might say that's weak. Rubbish. Unless they are making a complete nonsense of themselves and the situation, then I am more than happy to go with their thoughts particularly if they are along the same line as my own. You want to give them the best opportunity to do well and if you give them what they ask for they have no excuses. That's a big thing for me: no excuses. I think there are a few teams around the world who use that as their motto and I'm more than happy to make it ours. Prepare well, give people what they need and don't leave them the get-out of 'If only this or that had been different then I'd have performed.' I think that's the same kind of method that Sir Clive Woodward used in the Rugby World Cup with all his back-up staff. Our finances and budget aren't quite as extensive as his but we try to make it easy for the players so all they have to do is concentrate on playing.

During the one-dayers, I was delighted because I, too, was able to focus on my cricket, though that would change later in the summer. One down after Old Trafford, we won at The Oval, where young Jimmy Anderson polished off Pakistan for 185 with our first hat-trick in 373 one-day internationals. Tres, with a ferocious 86, and Vikram Solanki, with 40 not out, helped us to a comfortable seven-wicket victory.

It was very important for the team to get their first win of the series and for me to get my first as captain. It gave the young players confidence, as they realised they had beaten a very good Pakistan team on a very good wicket. So far I hadn't received any great stick in defeat or abundance of praise in victory.

It was becoming obvious that I was a little bit more laid back than Nasser and smiled a tad more. I knew there would always be comparisons with him because of the split captaincy. But my intention had always been just to be me; I wouldn't try to be anybody else. All I tried to convey was that we were enjoying it. I didn't want the players to see their leader stressed because if I saw my leader in that condition then I'd feel exactly the same. I always try to give an impression of calm and control no matter how I feel inside. For example, there had been a very tight situation in the first match against Pakistan and I'd had a giggle with Gough at the end of his run, just to try to relax him. I think little things like this are important. I didn't want him running in at that point tight and stressed, I wanted him loose and smooth.

Winning our first game, albeit the second in the series, was a massive boost for everybody. I'll be the first to admit now that when I looked at that Pakistan team I thought we were in a dangerous situation because you never know which of their two faces is going to turn up – the world beaters or the ones who couldn't beat a carpet. They can get 350 on any given day or be bowled out for 120. I didn't want to catch them on three of their great days because that would not have done much for our side's confidence.

To win at The Oval so convincingly set up the final game at Lord's on the Sunday as the decider. In one way we couldn't lose because a lot of the young guys would be gaining valuable experience of playing at the home of cricket in a crucial match in front of a full house. If we couldn't enjoy this then there was something wrong. We needed two or three players to produce something, something special. If that happened then we could end up winning the trophy. That would be an incredible success for such a young team.

We fielded brilliantly and when our bowlers got bashed around a bit towards the end of the innings, I didn't mind too much because it gave me a chance to see how they reacted when we were being kicked. To our credit, we did not back down. We restricted Pakistan to 229 for seven and the chase was on. I remember Shoaib bowling really fast; Trescothick and I shared a stand of 65 and we were cruising. Then I went and we had a string of accidents and near-misses. Chris Read went in when it was pitch black and desperately tense. But Trescothick flicked a decisive six with nine balls to spare, the final highlight of an unbelievable hundred. It was all over. We were the champions.

To win against Pakistan was an incredible turnaround. It

was a fantastic feeling to be on that Lord's balcony having won a series with a young, raw set of players. It had been refreshing to see our enthusiasm, particularly in the field, an area where English sides have not always been at their best – and that's an understatement.

It was as good a day at Lord's as I have ever had. I remember at the end standing up in front of the players and thanking them for their efforts, reminding them that they had achieved something really special by beating a very good Pakistan side. I also reminded them that the triangular series was coming up straight away. All the rewards and success of today would be forgotten if we didn't keep performing, and were not standing there in three weeks' time with another trophy. I said that if we showed the same enthusiasm, enjoyment and commitment in preparation then we could upset South Africa as we had Pakistan. I expected us to beat Zimbabwe, the third side in the triangular, but the South Africans were a very, very good one-day side.

Against Pakistan, Trescothick had played two of the best one-day innings you are likely to see. He had done it under me when actually he had wanted to be above me, to be captain. That's team-man Trescothick for you. I could feel a real buzz about the dressing room, a youthful exuberance and excitement. I knew as a developing team we would make mistakes, and nobody more than me. But we would enjoy the game and learn from our errors. However, I didn't want any of them to get carried away by being built up when we won. They would only let themselves in for being knocked over when we lost.

2

DOING IT MY WAY:
The 2003 NatWest Series

I am very critical of myself and I knew I had made mistakes. But Duncan is a good tactician and I used him a lot. Trescothick was at slip and Flintoff and Gough were also out there and I used their knowledge. In my early years with England, I hadn't been confident enough to offer advice to the captain; it was only after I'd established myself that my neck came above my collar. It had been different for others, the older, more experienced players, and I felt they could have helped more than they did. Nasser was very good on his own, but when we were under the cosh and trying to break up a big partnership, I felt that too many players, particularly senior ones, just hid in the field and didn't want to get involved.

I was never going to allow that to happen. I wanted all players involved at all times. It's easy when you are getting wickets and you are all flying around saying, 'Come on, have another slip,' or 'Put another man there.' That's easy. It's when times are tough that you still have to contribute.

But I was also trying to do it my own way: I was settling into my own style, a style different from that of some people I'd played under. Even after I got the job it never crossed my mind to read any books about the art of captaincy. I intended to sink or swim by my own method. Martyn Moxon was my first captain at Yorkshire. I was very young when I came into the side so all I can remember was being in awe of the whole team. I kept my head down, hardly saying anything and just playing my own game. Martyn's successor David 'Bingo' Byas was a very straight-talking, open, honest individual who could occasionally be aggressive. He was a tough man, who liked to run a disciplined ship; he wanted smartness and hard work on fitness. Discipline off the pitch breeds discipline on it: that was his philosophy.

I was different. There are players who you know will be on time, who'll be smart and won't need notes under their door to remind them of things. I am occasionally scruffy and forget details so I don't mind that type at all. The more different sorts of character, the better the group is. If we were all robots, stereotypes doing exactly the same thing, then it would be a very boring world.

My views on the need to reform county cricket were already getting stronger. Like the Aussies, we have to start producing players capable of coming into the Test side and scoring a century on debut. Bob Willis, Michael Atherton, Alec Stewart, Nasser Hussain and now me. We have all said exactly the same thing after taking over as captain and that is that the game's structure needs to be changed in our country. It's been talked about for 20 years and too many captains' heads have been banging on too many walls for far too long. I'm sure I won't feel the benefit, though hopefully my successors will.

It was only after I had experienced it myself that I fully appreciated what Nasser had been going through in his quest to drag England forward. Initially, I got involved in too many issues instead of realising different departments should look after themselves. I thought I could be a miracle worker and have a hand in everything, but it's not possible.

Part of the reason I overstretched myself was because the backroom work is vital. The staff behind the scenes don't get enough credit: they are as much a part of the team as the 11 on the field. As soon as we'd beaten Pakistan I complimented every individual on behalf of the players. The people who give us the stats, the video analysis, the physio work, the rub downs: they have to do just as good a job as the players on the field. I think we are one big unit or family. Everyone has to pull in the same direction. But it was not always easy. If I was going to ask the guys to work harder on their fitness then I had to do something about giving them a chance to let their muscles recover. We asked for a full-time masseuse. It would be a long time before we got one.

Finally, the team seemed to be responding to what I had told them: to go out and play, and not worry about the outcome. Just try and concentrate on the moment. The results will take care of themselves: if you start worrying and thinking about the result at 10.30 in the morning, you're not really thinking about the middle of the game, but the end of it, and there are dozens of contests to be won before that moment arrives. Focus on those contests and the outcome takes care of itself.

That is my theory anyway. The euphoria of beating Pakistan, however, quickly dissolved in the opening tri-nations when we lost to Zimbabwe. I wasn't overly concerned because given the inexperience of the team we were always going to have tricky days. It was inevitable. But already we were showing an ability to counterbalance the tricky days with terrific ones. At The Oval against South Africa, Vikram

Solanki hit a fantastic hundred in an opening stand of 200 with Trescothick, an England record, and we ended up beating a world-class side convincingly on a good wicket. My back had gone and I missed that game, but then a week later we went to Bristol, beat Zimbabwe and reached the final. Before that, we had to play South Africa again and we beat them at Edgbaston. What's more, we beat them batting second, under lights.

There was talk about huge disruption among the South Africans, that the captain Graeme Smith was a bit dictatorial, asking senior players to do things they had never done before, and that they weren't enjoying it. We felt we were meeting them at a good time and all the rumours added to our confidence. We'd beaten them by six wickets and four, which is very good at this level, and there was a real strut about the team.

We went to Lord's and produced one of England's best-ever one-day bowling performances. They were all out for 107. It didn't matter what I did, be it a bowling change or an alteration in the field, it seemed to work. You need a little bit of luck as a captain and I got mine that day as we won with ease to complete a special, special day.

It was a new team, but I still can't stand it when people ask if I thought it was 'my' team. It was new, it was young, but it was England's, not mine.

Nasser, of course, was still Test captain. I was in the corridor between the dressing room and the room where I had to do the press conference when my phone rang. It was Nasser and his message was simple and kind: 'Don't underestimate what you have achieved with that team.' His words were much appreciated.

3

TEST CAPTAINCY

Now it was back to Test cricket for the side – and back to the ranks for me. But as we headed to Edgbaston for the First Test against South Africa, the atmosphere had changed – and I think Nasser sensed it. I had led the team for three and a half weeks and more than half the Test team also played in the one-day side. I sensed that Nasser was just starting to think that a difficult situation was forming. He was probably saying to himself: 'Vaughny was telling them to do one thing two weeks ago and now it's me telling Vaughny and all the other guys to do something different.' You could tell he didn't feel as comfortable as he had in the Zimbabwe Test series when, although appointed, I still had not been in charge of the team. At that stage the players had not known my ways or my philosophies.

If Nasser had a problem with the situation, I certainly didn't because I respected his captaincy and certainly wasn't the type of guy to go around saying: 'If I'd been in charge, I'd have done this or that.' To me, that's the coward's way. I just wanted to focus on the job ahead and play as well as I could.

I could tell it was difficult for Nasser. We had a young

one-day team, a lot of lads whom I had just captained and had had a successful time with. I sensed a little bit of feeling that he had lost his team. They were still looking to me in the field. Throughout the game he wasn't his normal, intense, aggressive self or half as vocal as usual. He was almost relaxed on the pitch and that simply wasn't Nasser. Nervousness and intensity were what drove him on. He loved the edge. He liked shouting and giving everybody a kick up the backside – even if we didn't think we deserved one. He could go off at anybody, at any time.

There was none of that on the first day, which South Africa ended at 398 for one. Graeme Smith and Herschelle Gibbs put on 338, the best-ever opening partnership against England. Smith smashed us everywhere, and especially through midwicket. We didn't look a great unit. I'd come into the match struggling for runs and the first 20 I scored in reply to their 594 were probably the hardest of my life. I had to survive a very tough session from Shaun Pollock, not dissimilar from Australia's Glenn McGrath because of his consistency with line and length. The ball darted about here and there and at one stage I was on 12 for more than an hour, roughly the time Freddie Flintoff takes to hit a century. Then I came through it and played as well as I had for a while, pulling like I had in Australia the previous winter. I made 156.

Nasser scored one. I felt for him. It's horrible as captain when you don't get runs and you're still trying to demand the respect of your team. I could see in Nasser's face what he was going through. He had also gone very quiet. Either before the game or during it, he'd come to the conclusion that this was not his scene any more and that he'd had enough. I could fully understand his position. He'd had four years in the job and that's quite a long stint.

We avoided the follow-on and in our second time out in the field something changed or reverted. It was almost as if Nasser had decided that if he was going then he'd go in his own inimitable fashion, doing things the way he had always done. He shouted and gesticulated and his harangues were both collective and individual.

I could see the team thinking: 'Wait a minute, two weeks ago we had Vaughny in charge, not saying much until he felt it needed saying and definitely not flapping. And now we have Nasser shouting and ranting and generally right in our faces.' I had been convinced Nasser would see the series out. Now I wasn't so sure.

On the Sunday night, we hadn't seen him, which was unusual because he was usually around somewhere. When we arrived on the Monday there was a lot of talking in the coach's room. I could see Nasser on the viewing balcony with his head down and in his hands. I was chewing on a bacon butty when Duncan called me over and said Nasser was thinking about resigning. Was I up for the job if it became available? I immediately said of course I was, although realising these were far from ideal circumstances.

The next Test was to start in just three days' time and David Graveney said they would try to dissuade Nasser and encourage him to carry on. It became obvious during the day that he wasn't right. There were endless meetings and finally I was called in. Nasser came up to me and said: 'I want you to take the job on, I've had enough. I hope you don't think I'm leaving you in the lurch.' He said he'd seen what I'd done in the one-dayers and no longer felt it was his team, that it was mine. 'Good luck. I still want to be considered as a player,' he added, 'although I fully understand if you don't want me in the team. Just judge me on what I do in the middle.' I said: 'OK let's get on with it.'

Nasser thanked all the players for their efforts and for backing him over the years, but basically told them that he felt he had taken them as far as he could and that I could take them on. He asked them to give me the same commitment they'd given him. With that, everybody packed their bags in comparative peace and quiet. We had escaped Birmingham with a draw. Another era was over, a new one just begun.

4

NOW I AM THE ENGLAND TEST CAPTAIN:
Taking Over

I went out in Birmingham for a few glasses of wine when it hit me. I said to myself: 'Oh heck! I'm the full England captain. The captain of England. What position is the team in? What on earth has the game come to when I'm the England captain?' A little bit of self-deprecation never did anybody any harm.

It was strange for those in the team who had not been in the one-day squad and I could imagine them thinking: 'How do we react now that Nasser's gone?' I just told them I would see them on Wednesday and to be ready. But I feared that there was insufficient time. Definitely there was no real chance before the next game to put forward my views on the game and what I expected of the team.

I travelled down to Lord's on the Tuesday and as I pulled into a garage in Birmingham, just before I reached the pumps, I ran out of petrol. Two fellows were pulling in behind and they gave me a push for 30 yards. One of them looked at me and said: 'I recognise you,' and then he turned to his mate and said, 'Bloody hell, we're pushing the new England captain.'

We went to London and straight into a big game. I tried to say as little as possible because I just wanted the team to come through that match, somehow to pull out a performance in what were going to be tough circumstances. I had no problem with Nasser in the side because he was there on merit. I told him just to concentrate on his batting. I didn't know how difficult a week it was going to be for him, but I did know just how tough it was going to be for me. It turned out to be a hard week for everybody.

Nasser deserved his selection and had averaged nearly 40 in Australia. The selectors did ask me if I minded his being in the team and I could quite easily have turned round and said: 'I don't want him.' That would have been a weak thing to do. If he's good enough he should play.

So it was blazer on and out to toss. It was weird although I'd been looking forward to it. We were going to bowl, but they won the toss and stuck us in on a grey day. I wasn't too disappointed because it looked a good wicket. It was, but the ball zipped about and we didn't play well, getting ourselves out in all manner of ways. To be out for 173 when 350 to 400 was par wasn't good enough. My first day at the office wasn't quite as spectacular as I had hoped. In fact it wasn't spectacular at all. Darren Gough top-scoring with 34 had not been part of the plan.

Next day one of the lads handed me the *Daily Sport*, not my normal choice, which featured a very rude remark about me. I thought, I must have arrived!

We were always chasing the game. From a distance we must have looked in complete disarray and out of control.

Nasser dropped Graeme Smith on eight, a little dolly, and the South African captain went on to bat nine hours (it seemed like years) and make 259. Everything that could go wrong did. They amassed 682 for six declared and eventually beat us by an innings and 92 runs. The only good thing to come out of it was Freddie playing his first sensational Test innings at home. That was on the Sunday and it gave us a bit of a lift before the next game. We just didn't play well and our opponents showed better application and more determination. The entire team found it difficult, nobody more so than me. The players all wondered who they should be looking to in the field. There really hadn't been enough time to study things – especially Smith's quirky batting technique.

Out in the field – getting smashed everywhere and with no sign of a wicket coming – I started to wonder what on earth I had taken on. What was happening? I was hearing that Goughy might be retiring and that Nasser was thinking along the same lines. We were getting hammered in a Test match at Lord's of all places, two of the players might be retiring (Gough actually did) and we were struggling like hell. To add to the problems, Alec Stewart had gone off, Anthony McGrath had taken the wicketkeeping gloves and we were leaking byes. It was then that I started to see the funny side. The situation was like something out of Fawlty Towers. I simply could not stop laughing. Freddie came over to me. I had my Oakley sunglasses on and underneath I was laughing that much I was crying. He asked me what I was laughing at and I replied: 'Can't you see? Absolutely nothing else can go wrong so I might as well see the funny side.' It would have been useless to take it seriously because I knew I was in no position to do anything about it.

Afterwards, with the laughter long-since abated, I told the team that never again would an opposition side want to win more than we did. Of the things I would tolerate, that was definitely not one. I can accept that we will not win every game and there will be times when we are beaten, but that performance was unacceptable. I would never tolerate it again. I think they got my message. I am not a man of many words, but when I do open my mouth I want what comes out to have feeling and to be understood clearly.

I also told them that in future during games there would be no sitting in the back of the dressing room playing with bat handles. They would be out on the viewing gallery. I don't think the older brigade liked that because they didn't realise the importance their sitting on the balcony on public view has for a player trying to make a big score. I think they are wrong. The whole psychology of a team sport says that it makes a huge difference. They talk about it on television and nowadays I get letters saying your team look united on that balcony. I must have spoken for ages at the end of the game and it was almost a relief to get out of the ground. It had been such a tough week.

I took Nasser into a quiet room afterwards and told him in no uncertain terms that if he was picked for the next match, no way could he turn up with the downbeat attitude he had at Lord's. I told him to get it out of his system that he was no longer captain. He said: 'I'm sorry, I've been so unhelpful.'

I could understand why Nasser had behaved as he had. Emotionally it must have been very difficult for him, but I felt I had to tell him that if he did not sort himself out then there was no future for him in the team. If he did sort himself out then I wanted him. He totally agreed with what I'd said, which tells you a lot about the man.

I also asked Nasser what his plans were, just to set the record straight, and he admitted that although it had been a hard week he wanted to keep playing. As soon as he said that, then he was in the team. I wanted to use his experience, and to get him to pass on his knowledge to the rest of the lads, especially the younger players.

Nasser also gave me some advice of his own, encouraging me to get my presence over to the team. He knew it had been hard given the lack of time for preparation, but he felt it important that when we met up in Nottingham I put my philosophy over and let the side know what I expected.

We were in a poor position, 1–0 down to what was looking a very strong South African team, with three Tests to go. I went to Trent Bridge knowing it was going to be a massive game: if we lost, the series would have got away from us. If we at least drew it would give us confidence to move on. I knew my first day in Nottingham was going to be crucial. I had to convey my views about what I expected.

I had probably made mistakes but there weren't any huge blunders that I could remember. There is not a lot you can do when you've been bowled out for 173 in the first innings. Maybe in the second innings I got myself out in a frustrated manner because I had been disappointed in the way the team had played. I can also remember looking up at the balcony and there was not one person watching. That riled me.

I decided I would put over the same message I had given the one-day team. I expected a more professional approach to fitness; our trainer Nigel Stockill would be taking a more hands-on role and we would obey him. I wanted us more as a team, less as individuals – one for all and all for one. We would be training together, helping each other and not being shy. I said all this on the Tuesday, two days before the game.

On Wednesday I did the press conference which included the announcement that James Kirtley would be in the team for his debut, although the wicket would turn into the main talking point. It looked pretty good, but there was a suspicion that eventually it would crack and crumble. It did. Fortunately I won the toss and elected to bat. But I got out early to a good ball from Pollock. It was then that the two senior players in the team, Nasser and Mark Butcher, came to the aid of the younger ones and built a fantastic partnership. We needed Nasser's runs; we also needed his presence at the crease and he went out and chiselled a superb hundred. It was typical Hussain, full of grit and determination. You could tell by the way he celebrated – raising his bat several times to acknowledge a huge ovation – just how much it meant to him. It took a lot of courage which was again typical of the man.

We were the first to admit that we were lucky because on that first day the wicket was pretty flat. Second morning we went on to make 445, but by then the wicket was starting to show signs of deterioration. Then we got in among them. It was a relief to get Smith out – even though he had to tread on his stumps to help us – after his two double-hundreds, and we had them struggling before Neil McKenzie helped get them within 90 of us.

We had to bat for one over that night and Trescothick was out second ball. On the Sunday Pollock bowled well, we didn't bat well, the wicket was crumbling and we only scrambled a lead of 201. I remember a very irate Nasser going round the dressing room kicking things and cursing.

The culmination of a wonderful summer – the Ashes 2005.

What on earth has the game come to? My first press conference as England skipper.

A good day in June – England beat Pakistan in the 2003 NatWest one-day series.

Alec Stewart – a legend of the game.

Not a delegator – the buck stopped with Nasser.

Ray Illingworth was the only person to have a go at me before I started.

England has benefited from Mark Butcher's bulldog spirit.

Lord's rises to the South African captain Graeme Smith after his magnificent 259 in the First Test, August 2003.

Not bad, this job – chuffed to have beaten South Africa by 8 wickets in the Fourth Test at The Oval.

Graeme Smith turning the milk sour following the NatWest final at Lord's in 2003. England won by 7 wickets.

Combining swing and shooters, James Kirtley fires out Neil McKenzie at Trent Bridge.

A plan so cunning even we are completely demoralised – coach Duncan Fletcher, myself and Nasser prior to the Third Test against South Africa in August 2003.

In Kandy's hot and noisy stadium, we took the field first against Sri Lanka and I bowled my share of tweakers. We fought hard not to lose and the match ended in a draw.

Murali's controversial action – what do you think?

Staying focused during the First Test against Bangladesh in Dhaka, October 2003.

Ashley Giles appeals in vain in the drawn Third Test in Colombo – we couldn't stop the Sri Lankans building a substantial score.

Matthew Hoggard on his way to a hat-trick v. West Indies on the third day of the Third Test in Barbados.

For years, England lacked a genuinely awesome strike force. Now we have one – Hoggard, Harmison, Flintoff and Jones at Queen's Park Oval, Trinidad 2004.

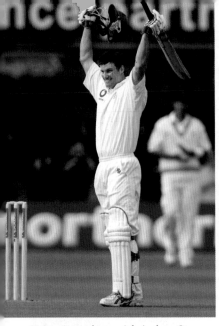

He's going to be special. Andrew Strauss waltzes to his debut Test century at Lord's against New Zealand, 2004.

The Kiwi all-rounder Chris Cairns bags Mark Butcher lbw in the Third Test at Trent Bridge, June 2004.

I could end up looking like this, you know. Captains in mufti – David Gower, Nasser Hussain, Bob Willis and Ian Botham.

It was obvious that he felt that we hadn't got enough runs and possibly that his first-innings hundred was going to be wasted. I was disappointed in his behaving in that negative sort of way. It was as if he was saying we'd lost already, when I felt it was far from over. I would not tolerate that kind of attitude and quickly put an end to it, telling the team: 'Look, they've still got to get the runs. This is far from lost on that track. Give it a go and don't worry about the consequences. Put the ball in the right areas, chase like border collies, and we still have a chance.'

We went out on the field and – I'll never forget it – they got off to a good start. We didn't make any early inroads and the crowd was clearly agitated. One section started singing: 'We all agree, Nasser is better than Vaughny.' I thought: 'Hell, that's a bit harsh. What have I done to deserve this? It's a bit early to be judging me.' I was convinced that we could still win. I remember saying to myself that the guys chanting for Nasser would probably be the first to sing my praises if we did turn it round. And by the close we had them five wickets down and the improbable was looking very possible.

I went to my room that night absolutely knackered. I knew just how big a game it was. South Africa needed 139 to win and I felt the following morning was going to be the biggest session of my career to date. It was crucial for the series, for me and the team to build confidence. I knew my detractors were still to be won over. They would have plenty of ammunition if we lost. I had to win their respect and also that of the public: they don't want to see a guy out of control leading the country. They want to see a guy getting things done and looking in complete charge.

Those thoughts were still churning in my mind as we

arrived at Trent Bridge for that final morning. I suppose a part of me was thinking that somebody was going to get them an 80 and win it, but I was not defeatist. Thankfully, James Kirtley produced a great spell – combining swing and shooters – and we won quite convincingly. The TV footage shows me celebrating their last wicket as if I had won the pools, Lottery and a Tote jackpot at Cheltenham all in the same day. And certainly I had been a bit lucky: I have not won many tosses, but that was perhaps the most crucial given the character of the wicket.

I didn't say much more than 'Well done' in the dressing room. I rarely say much after games, principally because I believe it pointless. It's best saving whatever has to be said for the next get together. Fletch was of similar mind. He just said: 'Great character, well done, build on that at Headingley.' That was it. It was enough. The players knew what they had achieved. They, like me, knew we were a side going forwards again.

The only thing I was feeling as I headed up the M1 for Sheffield was an overbearing sense of relief. We'd won a Test match ten days after looking unlikely to win one for ten years. We were tied 1–1 against a very good South Africa side, who would now be shorn of their best bowler Shaun Pollock for the next Test.

I'm always happy when I pass the sign which tells me I'm back home in Sheffield because it brings me back to reality. I can almost escape there because people have known me all my life and treat me just the same as England captain as they did when I was a Silverdale School pupil. I think they are proud that the England captain lives in their city, but I never get much hassle.

At home I'm a pretty ordinary guy. I love watching The Office or reading sports biographies. When my PlayStation whirrs into action it's usually to play Tiger Woods Golf. I'm a big Woods fan because I think he is the perfect role model – his hard work rewarded by a thousand titles. Another hero is Chris Waddle; I was lucky enough to play in the same Sunday league football team in Sheffield as him. I have great admiration for David Beckham, particularly after what he has had to put up with and the way he adapted so quickly to life with the galacticos in Madrid. It's not quite like that for me in Sheffield: I still have the same friends now as I had at school.

There are times when I reflect at home about how fortunate I have been to travel the world at somebody else's expense although I'm not a great one for sightseeing – preferring to discover golf courses in exotic places.

Now I had to concentrate on building a winning team.

5

THE SOUTH AFRICANS, SMITH AND SUCCESS:
South Africa 2003

It was with a feeling of huge optimism and relief that I arrived for the Fourth Test at Headingley. I got a great reception. I always have there – and there were plenty of good-luck messages. Although it's not always been a happy hunting ground for England Test sides, the Western Terrace (and now the Western Stand) always creates a great atmosphere and they do love their cricket. There would be plenty of banter, fancy dress and optimism.

I was confident we would repay them. Pollock had decided to return home to be at the birth of his first child. We were also at my cricketing home, where I felt we would have an edge. I thought we were in a great position to win.

It seems amazing now after what has happened since that we dropped Steve Harmison and brought Martin Bicknell into the team for his experience. At Headingley you have to put the ball in the right areas; spin doesn't play that big a role so we brought in Kabir Ali for Ashley Giles. We had them 140 for seven but from that point the game went away from us. Gary Kirsten was fantastic during his 130, the debutant

Monde Zondeki was infuriatingly streaky and South Africa were out of the mire.

Headingley can be one of the hardest grounds in the world to captain on. The ball beats the outside edge no end of times so you keep your slips in and have to leave gaps. You don't want to under-attack because you don't want the ball going through the air in catching positions. But if you do stray off line you can get punished. It can be a good place to bat because the ground runs away to the boundary and edges rush away for four. The sun comes out and the wicket is as flat as a crepe. Then all of a sudden the clouds come in, conditions change again and it starts to swing. These are the vagaries of Headingley, it's not always a place where bowlers dominate. You have to play to the conditions. I think I made a few little errors with field placings and the game began to swing away from us.

However, by the second evening it had swung back. We were 164 for one, with Trescothick and Butcher flying. Just 178 behind, I felt we could still win. It was at this point, when it was getting a little murky, that we were offered the light. They came off, Graeme Smith spoke 'a few harsh words' to his dispirited side and we lost the impetus, never to regain it. We were beaten by 191 runs. Looking back, it was the wrong decision. But it's stupid for anybody to say that I should have told our batsmen to stay out there. They were two senior players; they knew best what conditions were like and they were more than capable of taking decisions. Obviously, they didn't feel comfortable enough to carry on. If you go through life always looking for others to make decisions for you then you get nowhere.

I came out in the press conference after the match and

had a real go about the state of the county game. There were too many average-quality overseas players who could qualify through different channels. I would never be allowed to play in Australia or South Africa unless I was an official overseas player, so why were we letting it happen here? We needed to give all English players as much opportunity as possible. And the system bred too many players who were soft and fed up. I was just another English captain voicing the same old fears, but I felt I had to say something. It's a bizarre situation. It needs all 18 county chairmen to ensure change and those chairmen are not listening to the players at the top of the game.

I was gutted and just wanted to get things off my chest. It was my home ground, I'd had fantastic support and I felt I'd let people down. South Africa didn't have Pollock and I thought that should have been the difference because he'd have been a great bowler on that wicket. It wasn't that the hunger was missing from our team, just that our opponents played better. They grabbed hold of the game at key moments better than we did, which is something we have subsequently been able to do ourselves. Where there have been key sessions to win, we've won them more often than not and that's the key to beating good teams. A match generally comes down to one session and whoever dominates that session more often than not goes on to win.

We knew we had missed an opportunity. But I didn't let it eat into me. I'm a big believer in analysing mistakes, taking whatever positives are there and then moving on. You can't worry too much about the past because you can't influence it. You can fashion the future, however, and we were 2–1 down with just one match left. What happened at The Oval was a turning point for English cricket and for two players in particular: Harmison and Flintoff.

It would also be the last time that summer I would come into conflict with the South Africa captain, Smith. I'd never seen him play before he arrived and in the one-day series he looked unorthodox but effective; a big, strong, young man with good presence. He had assumed the captaincy in strange circumstances. South Africa had gone out of the World Cup in controversial style when Mark Boucher didn't quite understand the Duckworth/Lewis system and blocked the last ball of a match when they needed one to reach the next round. Captain Pollock got the blame – and the sack.

When South Africa came to England it looked like a camp that wasn't too happy. It was clear that the senior players viewed Smith as the new kid. I think he came in with almost a schoolboy-bullying style of captaincy where everything he said went and I'm not too sure some of the senior guys responded well to that. There were rumours throughout the one-dayers that they were totally uneasy with one another.

But I respected Smith. He had taken on one of the toughest jobs in cricket, was still only 22 and was opening the batting. He had inherited a volatile situation, particularly considering how much political wrangling there is in the way South Africa sport is run. And he quickly stamped his mark with double-hundreds in his first two Test matches here. When you do that as captain you soon command respect in meetings and your position strengthens. The respect he gained from those two scores was a huge thing for him and his team. Had he failed in those two games after the way he was leading his side, he would have been under enormous pressure. He could have been out of a job.

But there were a lot of questions still being asked about his captaincy. He certainly looked as if he was playing to the cameras in the field which is not something I'm keen on. Sometimes he appeared to have one eye on the job and the other on the big screen: every time his face appeared there he'd shout, clap and wave his arms, to look like he was the big man in charge. After every wicket he was the one celebrating most. It was as if he was saying: 'Look at me. I'm a power freak.'

Smith was in control of the series as both teams arrived at The Oval, but it was also Alec Stewart's last Test before retirement from internationals. I spoke on the night before the game, as I always do, saying that to lose to a good side like South Africa would not be a complete disgrace, but that it would obviously be a lot better if we drew the series. And then I let them ponder one thought. 'We owe it to Alec Stewart to make sure he ends his career on the right note. He started his career with a win, let's make sure the old git ends it with one.'

I remember when we went out saying to the team: 'Let's not die wondering what might have been, let's give it our all.' We did, but by late on the first day they were 345 for two. Finally we restricted them to 484; only once before in England had a first-innings total of 450 or more led to defeat. But it was a recovery of sorts and I thought we were definitely still in the game as long as we got somewhere near their total – and fast. It would then be a one-innings match.

We did it. Trescothick played the greatest innings of his career; Graham Thorpe came back into the side – it was good to have his experience after he had missed so much cricket – and made a hundred; and then Freddie came in with a very brisk 95 that gave us a lead of 120. That really kicked off Flintoff's run of incredible scores and it also tipped the balance of power our way, a fact acknowledged by South Africa afterwards. He provided the punch and changed the pace of the game, but Trescothick's double-hundred was the backbone. It was Trescothick's innings that allowed Flintoff to play freely and begin his remarkable run.

The making of Harmison was in the second innings. His length, rhythm and pace all came together at the same time. He had always been a player ready to explode – such natural ability with pace, bounce and swing. He could not have ignited at a better time for us. He started to threaten the best batsmen in the world as he brought the ball down from a great height with great heart and at above 90mph. His bowling on such a flat wicket was nothing short of unbelievable. He looked capable of rattling South African bones and wickets with every delivery and when he got rid of Jacques Kallis and Gary Kirsten it gave us a great boost.

I remember arriving on the Monday morning and realising it was going to be a special day in the history of English cricket. There would be a run-chase at some stage and it would be one we had to win. We rolled them over reasonably quickly, leaving us to chase 110. I went for 13 and then Trescothick and Butcher saw us home. It was one of our best Test victories for a long, long time. We had had criticism that we could not bowl teams out twice on a flat wicket and had exposed it as myth. It would not be levelled at us again after this mighty performance. To win on a proven flat wicket from a position where they had been 345 for two in their first innings was some effort. It was then that I realised we might be on to something good.

Without doubt, it was the making of Freddie and Harmy. Harmison had not enjoyed too much self-confidence, but you could tell by the way he came in and attacked that he was starting to believe in himself. Somebody with his ability was a very dangerous animal indeed and a weapon for any side. Harmison had gone into the match unsure of his future. He was wondering if he would be touring and whether he would get a central contract. I actually knew he was on the tour, but not about the contract because that was out of my control. He obviously put himself under pressure and that's what made his performance all the more significant. He's a quiet Geordie lad, pretty shy, but the better he's bowled the more he's come out of himself.

For us to finish that series 2–2 was an achievement which bordered on the unbelievable. It was one of the best series that had been played for a long time anywhere in the world given all the excitements both on and off the field. Viewing and attendance figures showed how it gripped the nation's attention. Smith must have left The Oval thinking: 'How the hell have we drawn that series?' They should have dominated the summer especially after going 1–0 up. From their position on day one they should not have lost a Test match.

We finished at 1.30pm and stayed in the dressing room until 6.30 drinking and enjoying our success. It was Alec's last day in international cricket and he had received an incredible ovation as he left The Oval for the final time in a long and distinguished Test career. I did want us to win that game for him, there was nothing false in that. No matter what you think about people, I don't like legends of the game going out on a low note.

There was still plenty for me to do before the day was over

including the customary press conference and a few meetings about who was going on tour, as well as the debate about whether Nasser should be included. Back in the dressing room, there was plenty of noise and singing, particularly in the big team bath. It was great to see Alec joining in for a change. It was not a customary sight because he normally kept himself to himself, alone with his thoughts and bottle of water. This time he entered into the spirit of things, probably because he knew it was the last time. We ended up playing football on the outfield at 4.30 with one of those big gym balls, using bottles of champagne for goalposts. You can imagine what state we were in by that stage. We were driven back to the team hotel and then to the official dinner. I remember Butcher being spectacularly relaxed and having to be taken home by the management, saying a few choice words to them on the journey to bed. I'm not sure he knew where he was or what he was doing, but they eventually got him to sleep. We went out clubbing and eventually retired at two o'clock having properly celebrated the victory.

The day after our Oval triumph, I had to help launch my first book. The signing was 200 miles away in Leeds and I was in a state when I turned up after the celebrations. Then, back home in Sheffield, it was time to reflect. I realised that my No. 1 goal before touring Bangladesh and Sri Lanka was to find some batting form.

My own brand of captaincy was developing, but I knew the finished article was a long way off. Indeed I could not be certain there would ever be one, although some ideas were working. My insistence on the team being energised on the pitch seemed to be paying off. We were fielding really well and there were plenty of good catches being taken. I knew we were not going to win every game no matter how good we were. We had played good cricket, but we were still miles and miles away from Australia's standard. There was still a long way to go.

6

BANGLADESHI BOOT CAMP:
Bangladesh and Sri Lanka 2003–04

I was getting better as a captain, but I still had much to learn. I hadn't scored many runs since I'd been handed the job and it kept being mentioned. I was getting 20s and 25s and playing iffy shots which I hadn't done for a long time. My rhythm had gone and my feet weren't moving. I was tired. Part of the reason was undoubtedly inheriting the captaincy. It was a daunting experience having the job thrown at me; I'd thought Nasser would continue through the summer, so mentally I was not quite ready for what happened.

My energies were probably going down the wrong channels – particularly in regard to meetings – and I didn't concentrate enough on what I do best: batting. I was getting involved in matters I shouldn't have been concerned with. There was a bit of the Macho Man about it: I wanted to change everything and do it my way. When you see things that aren't right you want to change them straight away, but you soon realise it's not possible. I didn't focus enough on practice in the nets. If

I got a low score, instead of going and working, I just thought to myself, don't worry, it'll come right in the next innings. I'm a big believer that the harder you work in the nets, the luckier you become in the middle and I probably didn't put in the hard work that I had previously. As time progresses, you begin to understand that even as captain there are only certain things that you have control of. I learned to try to control just what happened on the pitch. The other aspects of English cricket were hard for me to control and best left to others.

As soon as the summer finished, I made a pact with myself that my priority would be to make sure that I got my batting right. My goal was to get my form back in Bangladesh and Sri Lanka and become one of England's best batsmen again. I gave myself a good break because I was jaded. The pressures and unexpected developments of a hectic season had left me shattered. It was still a busy time because the final arrangements for my marriage to Nichola at the end of September had still to be sorted out. I admit to not having much to do with that side of the marriage; my biggest task was ensuring 40 mates and business colleagues made the flight to Spain for the stag do. We let our hair down for a few days and did nothing but eat, drink and be merry. Some were more spectacularly merry than others.

The wedding, attended by many of my England and Yorkshire colleagues, was in Sheffield and then it was on to the beautiful grounds of Chatsworth House in Derbyshire for the reception in a marquee, where Flintoff proved that he can bowl a decent line and length with a bread roll. An eight-day honeymoon in Dubai ended when the touring party had to get together for the journey to Bangladesh. I had deliberately not touched a bat between The Oval and leaving for Bangladesh. Now it was back to work and I went to see Duncan to deal with a few flaws that had crept in. The lack of practice would be put right now.

All the senior players who were available were selected to tour – there were no surprises. I have my say in selection, but I'm not a vote. David Graveney, Rod Marsh, Geoff Miller and Duncan Fletcher were the team selectors, with Graveney having the casting vote. My thoughts went through Duncan and we would always sit down and think things out before he went into the meetings. I believe it is important that the coach has more responsibility for team selection because he is the one who works with the players and who knows what the best XI will be in any given situation. I also think the captain and coach should get the players they want. We're the ones who get judged at the end of the day, when the newspaper stories get written. We take the criticism if things go wrong and we ought to take it on the chin – but only if we have what we want in terms of team selection.

Selection is important and for some time we'd been trying to bring more consistency. No matter what you are doing, if you are enjoying it then you do it better. If you are putting pressure, often undue pressure, on yourself then the likelihood is that you will underperform. There is enough pressure just playing international cricket without the selectors putting on any more. Some of the senior guys were a bit more wary of the new England and the new openness and honesty because they had grown up in a very tense international environment. It went back to the days before central contracts were introduced, where first and foremost you looked after No. 1 because you were just trying to get picked for the next game. There was no consistency of selection, there were no guarantees that you would get another bite. It wasn't the fault of our senior players; just the environment they had been brought up in. Today's cricketer has more time to impress.

We were now trying to build a county set-up within the England team: about 20–25 players with one another for long periods, keeping the squad together for practice days, trying to create that county mentality and team spirit where we all fight for one another. We were trying to create an ethic of team togetherness. Some of the older players were having difficulty adapting. They would soon be in for another shock.

Gym work had never been a huge aspect of English cricket and Graham Gooch was once considered almost certifiable because he ran and exercised. Everybody thought he was mad and asked why it was necessary to run to play good cricket. The longevity of his career should have given the answer to that one. Nowadays it's been proven that the fitter you are – the Australians and South Africans are all strong and athletic – the more physical you look on the pitch, and I believe that can give a team a huge psychological advantage. If you have a presence then you have an edge. We had also picked up too many injuries. I wanted the team to be fitter, stronger and able to withstand the inevitable niggles. I told Nigel Stockill, our physiologist, that I wanted the two weeks as we prepared to tour Bangladesh and Sri Lanka to be as hard a pre-tour as England had ever had. I knew the subcontinent would be the best place to do it because there are so few distractions; if you just sit in your room doing nothing it gets like Groundhog Day.

I don't think for the first few days we even picked up a cricket bat. We ran, swam, went to the gym, did weights, bleep tests, early-morning starts and pilates. We did the lot. This was our routine: early-morning breakfast, training, bit of cricket, fielding and fitness, dinner, rest, then into the pool for water polo. We filled the whole day with work on fitness. Some of the players had never done it before, especially the senior ones and I know they thought: What the hell's going on here? Because of the weather, we were travelling an hour and a half to have an indoor net, same time coming back, and within 20 minutes were thrashing about in the pool. I took some stick as did Nigel and there was a lot of singing at the back of the coach from the senior guys, mostly about being on the bus again. I'm sure they wondered what I was doing, and there was a bit of conflict but I didn't care what they thought. I knew it was for the best. After two or three days I think they started getting into it and the team ethic started to come through.

We'd place players of similar ability or fitness together, to work (or compete) with each other. Seeing Thorpe and Hussain training together a couple of times a day in the gym was an eye opener for us all. It became good fun. Players were beginning to realise the importance of fitness. That is one thing the academy has done, the one big positive: work ethic. Everyone who has come through it has developed a routine of gym, rehab, ice treatments, massage, fitness. It's second nature to them, but it was harder instilling it into the older players. We were playing a game and coming straight back into the gym. That's never been done before with England.

It was so wet in Bangladesh that we were having to practise indoors so it hadn't been easy to do what I had promised –

work on my batting. I had prepared myself mentally, however: a lot of batting is mental and a lot of my problems in the summer were caused by a tired mind. I went back to basics, worked as hard as I could so I knew I had given myself the best opportunity to succeed. I made sure there could be no excuses. I batted longer in practice and felt good in the warm-up games without actually getting many runs. Still, as one of my predecessors Michael Atherton was always fond of saying about getting runs in warm-up games, I didn't want to waste any.

The First Test in Dhaka was a funny environment to play in. Bangladesh had never won a Test and nobody wanted to be the first side to succumb. We did not know a great deal about them, but one thing was certain, there was plenty of noise at the ground. It was also the flattest of wickets and their captain, Khaled Mahmud, who looked about four foot six, came on first change and managed to nip a few back. There I was, trying to get back my form and I'm faced by something I had never encountered. It was the hardest bit of batting I had ever had to contend with – a bowler not bouncing the ball above shin height. I was batting four feet out of my crease knowing the only way he was likely to get me was lbw or bowled. I nullified whatever threat he may have posed yet I think he bowled five maidens on the trot against me. It took an age to get going, but once I got into my rhythm I was rewarded with runs.

When they had batted, Harmison carried on where he had left off against South Africa, and was a real threat, as he was always likely to be against short batsmen who don't really pull. He was getting it through on a flat wicket at chest high. We had restricted them to 203, but after Trescothick and I laid the foundations we crumbled and managed a first-innings lead of just 92. They were 153 on with six down when we arrived on the last morning. The match was delicately poised, but really we should have been hammering them. It didn't look like we could lose, but a draw would have been a magnificent result for them and a dreadful one for us. So there was pressure. We eventually needed 164 in 60 overs and managed it in plenty of time with just three down. I finished with 81 not out, which was a relief. It was also good to have Thorpe back, particularly on the subcontinent where he had enjoyed success. He seemed a more relaxed person now and he'd obviously found a new lady after all the problems with his marriage. He was very comfortable and happy. It was no surprise to see how focused he was; he had usually been that way – towards his own batting in particular. When he's in that mood you know there are going to be plenty of runs coming. We needed his experience because he's been through most situations on and off the pitch so the youngsters can turn to him for advice. He speaks in team meetings primarily about the mental aspects of batting.

The subcontinent is probably the hardest place in the cricketing world to succeed in. Everything is totally different, with flat wickets and weird environments. The routine is basically cricket and the hotel bedroom. At home there are no end of restaurants, cinemas, friends, places to visit: there's lots to occupy your time. Not there, so for young players it can be pretty daunting. I'd had six tours to the subcontinent so I was experienced, but not as much as Thorpe. He showed us the best way to play, how the sweep becomes a huge shot, and how important dinking the ball into the gaps and rotating the strike was.

As for Thorpey's mate Nasser, he'd looked very tense in his batting. He'd missed the last Test of the summer against South Africa with a broken toe and although he'd come to the celebrations on the night of that game, it was almost as if he felt he shouldn't be there because he hadn't been part of the victory. Nasser's a bit like that. If he's not playing he doesn't see the input he's had. Also he had been nervous about whether he'd be included for the trip because there had been rumours suggesting we were going to give opportunities to younger players. Hussain was tense and in the First Test he got very few runs.

For the Second Test we were in Chittagong which, without wanting to be too unkind, was probably the worst place I'd ever been to on an international tour. The hotel was very average and the electricity seemed to be on a half-hour meter – 30 minutes on, 30 minutes off. One restaurant wasn't too bad and having managed to keep down egg, chips and beans on the first night, we ventured no further down the menu for the rest of our stay. I was just hoping that the fact we didn't get the runs would not have cricketing parallels.

It was a very dull week – play, gym, egg, chips and beans, game of cards or PlayStation and bed. Surprisingly, the ground was not in keeping with the rest of the place, so at least we had the chance to enjoy the cricket in convivial surroundings. Bangladesh had missed their chance of drawing the game in Dhaka and I felt we would really make our advantage pay now. As soon as I saw the ball going through at decent pace, I knew our seamers would worry them, even though Harmison had gone home with a back injury.

His breakdown was something of a blessing in disguise because on his return he went to train with Newcastle United football club, saw at first hand just how hard Alan Shearer worked at his fitness and decided he'd better do the same. It paid massive dividends. Still it was disappointing when he left Bangladesh because he was becoming our senior bowler and there was speculation as to exactly why he had gone, given that his homesickness is well documented. But whatever the reason, it was the making of him. It opened his eyes and made him the bowler he would become in 2004.

I got another fifty and it was nice to have a consistent run going, while I was also encouraged by what I saw of the Surrey all-rounder Rikki Clarke, who looked as if he had plenty of talent. My second innings ended in frustrating if not unique circumstances, run out by my predecessor. Nasser knocked the ball into the covers and just ran. The umpire had his finger up before I was much past the middle of the pitch. I was a bit unhappy because it was common knowledge that Nasser is better at running to the other end than judging whether his partner also has a good chance of making it. He has been involved in a few run-outs and this was my turn.

It had no bearing on the result, however, because we won easily. It was encouraging as captain to get a couple of wins especially when my new ideas about fitness were only just beginning to have an effect. Changes to routine can backfire but they didn't and the senior players realised that this was the way it was going to be so they just went ahead and did it. It was pleasing.

Not everybody had an easy ride and Butcher was attacked in the press – an article insinuating that he was more interested in writing songs and playing his guitar in his bedroom than in scoring runs. It was less than accurate, but he hadn't got many runs and I think it hit home and hurt him.

It was a matter he would address after the one-day internationals.

We hammered Bangladesh by five or six wickets in every one-dayer, which reinforced my feeling that there wasn't much to be gained in those kind of games. The situation would later be repeated in Zimbabwe. I think we are degrading international statistics when players like Jacques Rudolph get 222 not out on debut against Bangladesh. Ten years ago would he have had to get that against the West Indies or Australia? I don't like international sport being degraded. I want to promote cricket in these countries because the more who can play the better, but there could be another tier for them just below full international level. A year later, before our tour to Zimbabwe, we prepared against Namibia and the two one-day games we played against them were as hard if not harder than the ones on the official tour. Zimbabwe could actually put out a good team, but they cannot do so for political reasons. However, Bangladesh just don't have players good enough for Test cricket. Until they have, I don't think they should be allowed to compete at the highest level.

So to Sri Lanka, where I'd made my one-day debut. I knew it was going to be a big test because playing there is totally different from what we are accustomed to. Sri Lanka is a very mentally draining place to bat in because it's so hot, the close fielders are in your ear all the time and you know that to score runs you're going to have to face and block a lot of balls especially against Murali. Also there were going to be more than 90 overs bowled in a day because of the spinners' fast over rate. It was going to be a good chance to test ourselves, but during the one-dayers the rain didn't allow us the opportunity. Most of the time we just watched thunderstorms and when we played at Dambulla, we lost.

I got criticised by our supporters because there were rumours that we had called off one of the games in Colombo. That was absolute rubbish because the pitch was like a bog and not fit for international cricket.

We all enjoyed watching England win the Rugby World Cup and we were scheduled to play the following day. While warming up in bright sunshine I said to the lads that it looked like we'd be starting on time. Just as I said it the groundsman came on with his hat on, asking all his staff to get the sheets ready. There was the smallest cloud you have ever seen about a mile away and he said: 'You won't be tossing up because there's going to be an almighty storm in about five minutes.' I thought he'd lost his marbles. Five minutes later, we watched the mother of all storms turn the pitch into a lake.

The Test players then arrived, including Butcher who had a focused look on his face. It had been mentioned that Andrew Strauss was waiting to take his place if he didn't improve his attitude. It obviously worked as a kick up the backside for him because throughout the Sri Lanka tour he impressed. We were without Harmison which was a pity because I remember Andrew Caddick in 2000–01 having got a bit of life from the Sri Lankan pitches with his extra height. We were missing his firepower in an incredibly hard place to go and win. It is also a place, however, where if you can get your opponents under pressure on days four and five, they seem to feel it more than most teams. The Sri Lankans don't seem to deal with pressure in their own backyard, probably because of their fanatical supporters.

Nasser pulled out on the morning of the First Test at Galle

with a mystery illness and that gave Paul Collingwood a chance. We ended up playing a good game and drawing. The toss, always important, went their way, but Giles – who bowled really well – and Gareth Batty wore them away in the second innings to leave us a victory target of 323. It was never really likely and Hoggard, a useful blocker but not the man you would chose in such circumstances, had to see off a final over from Murali. We celebrated as if we'd won because not to lose in Sri Lanka when you've lost the toss is a huge result.

The thing that stood out was that their captain Hashan Tillekeratne was very negative. He had the world's best spinner and was playing with a sweeper on both sides of the wicket; he never tried to get us hitting Murali over the top. I found his captaincy throughout the series bizarre. It may have been because he was under pressure, or it could just be the way he plays the game, but we thought he made a lot of errors.

It was the same in Kandy. Eventually we were left an unlikely target of 368. Their coach, John Dyson, kept saying that we were playing negatively, but I would have liked him to have told me how to score 3.5 an over off Murali when they had all their sweepers out on both sides of the wicket. There were three catching and the rest out, so there were no boundary options and it's just as difficult to hit Murali for ones as fours.

The match was personally memorable because I nudged, drove, pulled and cut my first century as a captain. It was a huge moment for me, especially considering that to draw the game we'd had to bat out 108 overs, with Murali coming in remorselessly from one end all day. The longer you spend out in the middle, the more confident you become and the easier it is to face him – although it's never exactly a doddle and my century took more than seven hours. It was my best Test hundred.

The match was not without incident as Nasser, back in the side when we'd decided to pack the team with batting, decided to unleash years of pent-up emotion and frustration by calling Murali a chucker as he came out to bat. Around the international circuit there is a strong band of opinion which suggests he chucks the ball. I'm not sure, but if he does then he throws it very well indeed. His new 'doosra' ball that went the wrong way was getting us out for fun and Thorpe, who had had a great tour three years previously playing against his orthodox off-spin, was finding it almost impossible. It was the same situation with Trescothick, another great player of spin. There were people who thought that this new doosra was merely a new way of chucking it.

Nasser must have been frustrated that Murali was still playing the game and let it get the better of him. When somebody abuses me on the pitch I just let it wash off, but Murali went running off complaining to the match referee. I wasn't impressed. If you get a bit of stick you don't have to go running to the headmaster, but the Sri Lankans seem to do it on a regular basis. We're called the whingeing poms, but I can tell you we're a long distance second to the Sri Lankans.

We had a great team spirit developing and we'd gone to Kandy feeling we would fight like anything to get something. We knew it would be a battle to ensure we didn't lose, that we would have to draw on the bulldog spirit in hot, humid and noisy conditions. Our commitment was incredible.

We then travelled to Colombo for the decider, a three-and-a-half-hour coach journey. We sang all the way, enjoying a few beers along the road with Thorpe and Freddie in the back of the bus in fine form. That was more than could be said for Flintoff on the field. He had been struggling with Murali, who had claimed his wicket a couple of times with few runs against the Lancastrian's name. Before the final game he practised for hours. He worked and worked and worked on his technique while people sent down off-spinners at him in the nets.

Colombo was always going to be tough as soon as we saw the wicket. We won the toss, batted and reached 100 without loss after 20 overs. Trescothick smashed them everywhere, but then we lost a stream of wickets and 265 was never going to be anywhere near enough. They got millions. If we looked a jaded team in the field it was nothing to how we appeared after Sri Lanka finally declared on 628.

It was as if all the matches had been rounds in a prize fight and they'd finally backed us against the ropes. We were facing rounds eight, nine and ten and we'd been taking punch after punch. Finally, painfully and unequivocally they were knocking us out. Counter punches were few and far between.

Murali had a field day, while Charitha Buddhika Fernando was hitting a length and causing a few problems. We missed having somebody to back Flintoff up and they eventually knocked us out. We lost the match by an innings and 215 and the series 1–0.

I was still very proud of the team and told them that there was no reason to be discouraged. We fought so well with everything against us, but just took one hit too many. We had plenty to take away as consolation, because we had competed despite facing Murali on difficult wickets and missing Harmison's firepower.

Not everybody viewed our series defeat quite so philosophically. We had a makeshift Christmas party in Colombo and an England supporter came up to me and said: 'You guys seem to be celebrating a defeat.' I told him we were not celebrating, we were together as a team and at the end of a series that's what we did, win, lose or draw. What he did not appreciate was how much work we had put in. We had got to the last Test before we folded – lesser sides would have gone down earlier.

I felt it important that we got together to have a drink in the bar. There were cliques in the England dressing room when I first opened the door. You have your friendships, your closer friends, but you have to pull together as a team. It was a 7pm meet, but Thorpe and Nasser did not show up until much later. They obviously didn't believe that occasional togetherness off the field as well as on it helps to create a winning team.

7

CARIBBEAN CRUISE:
West Indies 2003–04

The tour to the Caribbean after Christmas was going to be a crucial one for the team and for me. We were quietly confident that after the holiday period we would be able to get our minds and bodies right for what was going to be a serious examination. I was enjoying the captaincy, going so far as to describe it as fun. I had found it difficult in Sri Lanka, but then so does everyone. There is a lot of pressure as captain, not least because your mind is distracted towards other areas rather than just being team leader. I tried as best I could to put all those aspects to the back of my mind and concentrate on the main role. That's actually easier when you are out of England. At home, there are so many different things that you can get involved in, but abroad those issues aren't there.

Looking back, the only person who had seriously had a go at me was Ray Illingworth, a predecessor at Yorkshire and England. He's written that he thought I was not strong enough to be captain. I couldn't believe it. From somebody who had played for my county I would have expected support rather than criticism – at least until he properly saw how I was getting on. He didn't know me or what I was like, he'd never been in my team's dressing room and yet he felt knowledgeable enough to comment.

How can you offer a full opinion of somebody when you don't know him? When it comes from somebody who knows you and has played with you, then you have to accept what they say, but for somebody of yesteryear who had never met me? Maybe he needed a few extra bob for a column. I don't know what it is, but Illingworth seems to have a grudge against any player from Yorkshire who gets into the England team. Something similar happened between Fred Trueman and Darren Gough, and it's disappointing. One thing I will never do is criticise younger players when I've finished playing.

I find Illingworth sad. I very rarely read a positive piece he's written about cricket and yet here's a man who made his living from it. His day has gone and he really has to look to the future. I respect what he did as a great captain and a good off-spinner and he probably thinks he knows me, but he has never seen me in the dressing room or heard me give a team talk. That's where I do the talking. That's where he would see I am a bit harder than he thinks.

There was quite a lot of debate initially about my style of captaincy and maybe Illingworth saw it as a weakness that I didn't wave my arms around and give on-field dressing-downs. I understand that a bowler can bowl a bad ball and the last thing he wants is to see his captain with his head down, shaking it and waving his arms. That's just not me and I'll never do it. If I'm going to give a dressing-down, I'll do it in my own space where others don't see it. A lot of shouting and bawling is just for show.

Other than Illingworth the press had been pretty fair although there are always things written that you disagree with. I don't read a lot of newspapers. I'll just see the odd snippet here and there in different papers, but there isn't one I would buy regularly. You have to realise as England captain that you will make decisions and that those decisions are going to be analysed. As long as the comments are fair then I never complain. I'm a bit similar with the television coverage. I don't really listen that much to the commentary. We have the pictures but not the sound on in the dressing room. If the players want it on they can have it, but more often than not it's off because what's said can affect or influence the listener. It's not too bad if it's complimentary, but adverse comment can affect a player's psyche and that's no good. You never know whether it's going to be praise or criticism so it's best not to have the sound on.

With the bat I was not quite back in the form I showed in Australia because that period had been a golden one. Ask any cricketer and he will tell you that there may be two of those peaks in your career, if that. Alec Stewart told me there were a couple of occasions when he enjoyed similar success and that the rest of the time was back to normal.

Selection for the tour was tricky. During the last Test in Sri Lanka there had been a debate as to whether we'd go for Nasser or Collingwood and we opted for the former. He didn't do that well, but there were other considerations to take into account. Again the selectors finally went down the route of experience – although Collingwood made the squad – because we didn't know how well an inexperienced middle order would do, whereas the likes of Nasser, Butcher and Thorpe had all played in the Islands before. We thought their knowledge might be crucial and we were proved right.

It was perhaps fitting that Simon Jones came back into the

squad because his father Jeff had been part of the last England team who had won in the West Indies in 1967–68. Simon had been preparing with the Academy team and once his fitness was assured he was always going to come back because he can menace batsmen – as he had proved in Australia before he sustained his horrendous knee injury. It was a delight to have him available again.

Harmison also returned and looked in fantastic shape. He had been training with Newcastle United, the football team he had supported since he was a kid. He idolised them. Seeing how Alan Shearer worked out was a real eye-opener for Steve. It hit home to him that he was these guys' equivalent and if he were going to endure then he would have to work to a similar standard. He went there day in, day out and was in superb condition by the time we set off.

He was fit, his back was fixed and he was ready. Nobody could have guessed quite the impact he would make, but I had a sneaking feeling that something special was going to happen. Everything about his work ethic seemed to have changed. He'd still be at it after a long, hard day in the field and I'd never seen this from him before. We have Alan Shearer to thank because I always knew that if Harmison's work-rate ever matched his talent then he would be an incredible performer.

Like Steve, we were all being expected to work and train harder, but I felt that although we were pushing our bodies, there was nobody there at the end of the day to give a rub-down. The ECB told us that there was no money in the budget for either a masseur or masseuse, so we decided to fund one ourselves. The ECB eventually saw how useful the masseuse had been and she is now a full-time employee.

Since getting back from the subcontinent I'd done very little to keep fit. I'd stayed at home most of the time, had a short trip to Ireland to see Nichola's family, watched a bit of Sheffield Wednesday and Manchester United, played a few rounds of golf, attended a couple of dinners and enjoyed the odd night out, I'd also done a few question-and-answer sessions, though I'm not into after-dinner speaking.

As we boarded the plane and I prepared to catch up on some sleep, my favourite flying pastime, we all realised we had a wonderful opportunity to make history. We all knew the Caribbean was going to be a huge stepping-stone in the development of a new England squad. We hadn't won there for 36 years, but they had an even younger team than us and we felt that maybe this would be our chance, even though the presence of Brian Lara would always make it difficult. We were in good heart knowing that the West Indies is a great place to tour – more relaxed than most places although always tense on the pitch.

For the first week we were based in Jamaica's capital Kingston – an interesting place – and we knew what to expect. Three or four local lads would all be trying to knock our heads off in the nets while there would be guys sitting in the stands commenting on every shot and warning us that once the Tests started we could expect some serious 'chin music' – as they like to refer to short-pitched bowling. But it was good-natured banter in the net sessions and any batsman pulling or hooking would get a standing ovation.

We worked very hard leading up to the First Test, including having team meetings where we set goals and debated how we were going to achieve them. These were the team objectives, but it was also up to individuals to set their own.

It was something Duncan and I had been talking about for a while and this was the first time we had put our ideas into operation. We thought that since this was going to be such a good trip, it would be an ideal opportunity to introduce this goal-setting agenda.

We also had time to relax and Vodafone fixed up a golf match against the media which we won convincingly. Ash and I took on David Lloyd from the *London Evening Standard* and Sky's cricket producer Barney Francis. It was no contest really, but a lot of fun. Back in the middle, we won a three-day game in two against the University of West Indies Vice-Chancellor's XI on a pitch that was best described as average. That's one thing about the Caribbean – you can never guarantee the quality of the facilities and this pitch was very dubious.

The first thing I noticed about the West Indies is that time is never the essence. I can't remember ever seeing a clock. The locals are cricket mad, maybe not as much as they were in the '70s and '80s, and they really let you know what you can expect. 'Tino Best and Fidel Edwards will be giving you the chin music, man', 'Lara's going to smash Harmison all over the place' – that sort of thing.

Abroad, I always like to go native when I can and our security guard took me out in his car through the streets of Kingston. It is not an exercise I would recommend unless you are inside a Chieftain tank. Seeing the gangs on the street corners was a little unnerving although I felt much safer visiting Bob Marley's house, now a museum to the man and his music. The welcome party was a guy with a big spliff in his hand offering directions to the wonders within. It was fascinating, particularly since I enjoy museums and the homes of the famous, Sir Don Bradman's being one I visited Down Under. I got a real buzz about Jamaica and could sense how special it was in cricket history.

My job had been made easier knowing that the work ethic I'd insisted on had been adopted by everybody. They were all working hard without my having to get on to them. At the end of my first season in charge, I had written a letter to each player, a thank-you for all the hard work they'd done. To a man they responded positively.

We knew it was going to be noisy when the First Test started because our dressing room is directly beneath the Mound Stand, sponsored by Sandals holiday resorts where, for £50 a day, you can enjoy as much beer as you want while scantily-clad young ladies from the resort act as cheerleaders. Brits and locals all congregate there producing a weird atmosphere. As more beer is taken on board, the remarks increase and become bawdier and every ball is commented on.

My opposite number was Brian Lara, but I'd seen him only as a batsman, not really as a captain, so I wasn't sure what to expect. There had been rumours that their camp wasn't happy and that certain players were causing problems. They had just toured South Africa and got walloped so there were plenty of stories in the papers about whether Lara should be captain. All we knew was that he was their best player and most senior one, so if he had other things on his mind then all well and good. Anything that might nullify his threat to us, I'd go along with, so it was nice to have him under as much pressure as possible.

Apart from Lara, Shiv Chanderpaul, Ramnaresh Sarwan and Chris Gayle, the rest were raw and inexperienced although talented. We'd heard that Tino Best was a bit of a loose cannon, but we had little idea what to expect of Corey Collymore and Fidel Edwards, who would be quick. In short, we didn't quite know what we would face. We had plans for every player, but could not be absolutely sure that we were on the right lines because we knew so little about so many of them. Edwards we knew was short for a fast bowler with a slingy action, could move the ball away, would be dangerous with the new ball and could get reverse swing. Our information on all the other newcomers was sketchy to say the least.

They won the toss, batted and made 311. In reply, Best and Edwards proved as quick an opening pair as I had faced and the crowd was going ballistic as we crumbled to 33 for two. The supporters had been crying out for some new fast bowlers because Courtney Walsh and Curtly Ambrose had never been replaced, indeed some considered them irreplaceable. The crowd really gave it everything and the bowlers came tearing in. I expected them to be quick, but not that quick. However, Butcher and Nasser then put together an incredible partnership. They put on 129 and we clawed our way into a first-innings lead. It was the two experienced heads who made the difference between us winning and losing so I'm sure the selectors were delighted. Sticking with experience was a crucial decision.

We had them on the rack and particularly Lara, thank heavens. We'd spoken about how he looked a little uneasy when the ball was coming across him and Simon Jones in the first innings and then Hoggy in the second undid him with balls which did exactly that.

But it was Harmison who stole the headlines and quite rightly. Without doubt, he produced the best fast bowling I had ever seen. Pace, swing, bounce, accuracy: he had the lot and West Indies had very little to respond with. I'd always known he had that raw potential, but this was not potential, it was reality: seven for 12 and West Indies 47 all out, their lowest-ever Test score. It was fantastic and I had eight slips at one point. It wasn't showing off or trying to intimidate them. I just could not see the ball going anywhere else but that area. There is an old adage – you work hard and you get your rewards, and Harmison was definitely getting his. It was superb because it really looked like we had unearthed a major weapon. Hoggard, Jones and Flintoff also bowled well and we had a four-man pace attack very reminiscent of those which touring teams used to face when travelling to the West Indies. We won by ten wickets, the match turned in half an hour of some of the most devastating fast bowling ever witnessed. It was so satisfying. It's a great feeling as a player when you win, but it does not compare with the huge pride you feel when you win as a captain.

It was a strange match really because there was a time when it looked like West Indies might sneak it and if they had I am sure we would have seen a more confident team for the rest of the series. They did not take their opportunity, we did. I thought we might win the series before we came out. I now knew we could and Lara's men were dejected.

I'd never been to Trinidad before and I remember thinking how much character the place had, with a continuous carnival atmosphere. In a fascinating diversion we were invited to Brian Lara's hilltop retreat – the home he built on the land given him after he scored 375 in 1994, the innings that broke Sir Garry Sobers' Test record. Inside, the house reminded me of a kind of American bachelor pad with every gadget and mod con imaginable.

Back at work, I remember thinking as soon as I saw the wicket at Port of Spain that there could be plenty of bowled and lbw's – line and length would be the key. The team was not an issue, with no changes from the one that had performed so heroically in Kingston.

The only problem I foresaw would be with one of the sightscreens. It was not quite high enough and we would have difficulty picking up their left-armer, Pedro Collins, so we asked them to make the necessary adjustments. Little details like this can make a big difference.

It was, by now, becoming predictable that I would lose the toss and I knew before Lara's words were out of his mouth that we would be asked to field. The pitch looked to have plenty of runs in it, flat and slow, and my feeling was reinforced when Chris Gayle helped smash us for 100 in the first session. I had a feeling we would be chasing leather for a long time and might be looking at a total of 500.

Then, just before lunch, I put Harmison on at the end with the dodgy sightscreen and he ripped into them. From a dominating position they were suddenly four down – and one of them was Lara. It totally changed the game, which began to pivot our way.

The wicket started nipping around and seaming from nowhere – and I got a duck – but Butcher, Hussain and Thorpe repaired the damage. The England support, always vocal and often entertaining, was incredible. Port of Spain is a real bowl of a ground, similar to a cycling track, and the atmosphere was really, really good. We were determined to give them something to cheer about.

If we have a chance to win early I will always go for it, so when we needed less than 100 with 18 overs left on the fourth day, I told the lads I wanted it finished that night. I did not want to risk losing a day to the weather or the chance to go 2–0 up in the series. We did it, earning a day off while Mick Jagger took some of our other squad members out partying.

From them being 100 for one on the first day, this was a big result for us. Rod Bransgrove, chairman of Hampshire, had a yacht in the Caribbean and every time we won he invited us on to it. We were regular visitors. Wine, jet skis, speed boats, you name it, we enjoyed it as we sang and drank to our latest success. We had expected to play well in the Caribbean, but had not thought we would be 2–0 up after two Tests or to play the standard of cricket that we had.

It would get no easier for West Indies because we were heading to Barbados knowing that we would have thousands of supporters there, including our families. There was a two-day game in between the Tests and it was decided that I would rest even though I hadn't been in good touch. The wickets had been tricky for batting on, but something wasn't quite right, and for a few days I played golf, spent time on the beach, relaxed at the health spa and basically chilled out. There is no place on earth like the Caribbean for doing that.

Thousands of our supporters turned up just to watch our practice sessions. Everywhere you travelled there were St George's flags and people wearing England shirts. You knew it was going to be something special. I think the ground holds about 18,000 and there was talk of there being 16,000 Brits.

There was also talk about Geraint Jones coming in for Chris Read as wicketkeeper, but we wanted to give Read another go, to give him an opportunity to score some runs.

There was no doubting his wicketkeeping credentials, but these days a player coming in at No. 7 must be able to contribute reasonably well to the run total. Geraint had pushed his cause during the two-day game and looked ready for international cricket. Other players had noticed it too. David Graveney came out to Barbados and we had a bit of a chat there about it, but eventually we ended up going in with the same team.

Surprise, surprise, we won the toss. We put them in because it looked like there was a little bit of life in the pitch which we might be able to exploit. A local Rastafarian had told us about the wisdom of always bowling first in Barbados because there was juice in the early-morning wicket. The public there tend to be very knowledgeable about the game; a little bit like Scots and golf. We'd be in a restaurant and a waiter would come over and start talking cricket. Soon enough, he'd be telling us how to get Gayle out, how to get rid of Lara, how to play Collymore. This particular dread-locked sage said if you bowl first then you can get the opposition out cheaply. He wasn't wrong. We fielded well, the ground was full of Brits and this was the first time that I had ever seen one arena dominated so much by away supporters.

Flintoff bowled as quick as he had for a long time, Thorpe made a revitalising century and by the end of the second day we had got Gayle out twice.

The next morning we just snatched the game away from the West Indians. Hoggard got a hat-trick and the roar was unbelievable. We had to chase down 93 and I wouldn't have wanted it to have been more. We set about the task in typical Trinidadian fashion and smashed the ball unmercifully.

Anything like 180 on a tricky wicket might have been a different proposition. Every time they got on top of us, we had fought back. When the situation was reversed, we nailed the advantage down. As *Wisden* later recorded, this was the precise opposite of much of England's recent cricket history. We were going in the right direction.

The scenes that followed were like nothing I had ever seen. There were 80-year-olds singing, kids dancing and, as always with the Barmy Army, plenty of lager. We couldn't go anywhere for days without people wanting to buy us drinks. It was a non-stop English party for two days, but the West Indies were gracious in defeat, particularly Lara, who is a friend, a legendary player, and also a good man.

The West Indies had experience, but also looked brittle among the inexperienced. We always knew if we could get Gayle and Lara early then the rest might succumb to the pressure. With the slightest shove, the dominoes would fall. None of them was playing that well – including Lara, as we kept getting him out cheaply. His day was still to come. Their bowlers might have been fast, but Best and Edwards were also raw. Pedro Collins and Collymore were honest enough, but outgunned by Harmison, Flintoff, Hoggard and Jones – all firing and showing pace and aggression on quick wickets which suited our style.

The party mood would quickly dissipate when we arrived in Antigua. We had a stressful few days when nobody was happy, with players wanting to move out of our hotel. Too many of the Barmy Army staying there wanted to sing when we wanted to sleep and we should not have been in that kind of environment. At the ground, the practice facilities were far from ideal and there were ructions in the camp. Meanwhile, West Indies had prepared a pitch which would counter any thoughts of us getting a whitewash. A pancake could not have been flatter had a ten-ton steamroller gone over it a thousand times.

There was more controversy about our team selection as we picked Geraint Jones ahead of Read. It was a bit harsh but we just wanted to extend our batting into the lower order. The selector Rod Marsh didn't agree with it and there was a lot of flak flying around in the media particularly as it looked as if our decision had flown in the face of selection protocol. It is different now because the selectors pick the squad and team for the summer series, while for winter tours they give you the squad and Fletcher and I pick the XI. Then, it was the selectors who should have picked the team in winter and summer, so Mr Marsh wasn't happy.

It was a decision we did not take lightly. We consulted senior players and everybody agreed that Geraint looked so special that he would break into the team at some stage, so why not sooner rather than later. The series was won so we decided to have a look at him.

When it happened, an MCC team (effectively an England A side) were playing under Marsh at Lord's and he saw it on teletext. He went berserk in front of all the players, abusing England's cricket, captain and coach. Whether you like the decision or not, that was not the right kind of response.

We made the decision because we felt we had to and looking back we may have done it in the wrong fashion. We could have talked more to the selectors, but they weren't there so we had to deal with it and I'm glad we did. I went and saw Read and told him there was no criticism whatsoever about him as a keeper, but that we saw Geraint as somebody who could get us a century from No. 7. It wasn't necessarily the end of his England career; all we were doing was giving Geraint an opportunity. Jones's positive attitude towards the game is special and that's what I like about him. Also his thought processes on the pitch mark him down as a clever thinker and he has been a great help to me.

As it turned out, we had plenty of time to examine his keeping, or would have done if anything had got past the bat. West Indies won the toss and the only things I can remember after that were: one, that we felt we had Lara caught behind before he'd scored, and two, that once he was given not out he never looked like getting out. The rest is blanked out. He ended the rain-interrupted first day 86 not out and when we left the field that night I was already thinking that Matthew Hayden's world-record 380 would not last another day. It did, but not a second.

It seems a little strange, but a few of us, when 400 came into Lara's sights, were actually willing him to do it. The sheer majesty of it all had been a marvel to witness. He hit boundaries at will and I'm sure Ashley Giles, who missed the match through injury, was not that unhappy. Hoggard went down ill so that made us a bowler light, but we could have included McGrath and Murali and it wouldn't have made a difference.

When Lara is in that kind of mood, the only thing capable of getting him out is a missile. He gave a half chance on 293 before finally beating the record ten years to the week after he won it first. The game stopped, the president walked out to pay homage and we all added our congratulations. He had actually done us a favour because if he'd wanted to win the match he would have declared long before he did, but he did put the whitewash beyond our reach. We knew we would have to bat for the rest of the game.

Flintoff dragged us out of serious trouble with a fine hundred, but we still had to follow on, although they didn't have the firepower to get us out a second time on that pitch. I was happy to finish the tour with a big hundred because it had been a tough series for the opening batsmen with the new ball darting a bit most of the time.

I've always got on well with Lara and played a bit of golf with him. We certainly didn't begrudge him the record even though we would have preferred a whitewash. We all became fans for the moment as he signed our tickets, bats, shirts and anything else we could get our hands on. He's taken a lot of criticism as you do when you are captaining a losing side, but often there isn't much a captain can do. A lot of what he was being criticised for was outside his control.

Lara had a young team and it's tough in the West Indies because they don't play much first-class cricket, so they are basically learning the art of the game in the Test arena – and that's not easy. We're quite fortunate in that, whatever else is wrong with domestic English cricket and its structure, we still have a good learning ground. Players play with a county for three or four years and learn the basics.

I'm sure Lara got very frustrated at having to teach people in the Test matches – and I'm talking about the real basics such as running between the wickets. That can't be easy. Things can be difficult for any captain in the West Indies. Bags don't always arrive when you would like them to, practice facilities aren't great, surfaces aren't that good and the net bowlers have their own schedules. They turn up if they have a mind to and occasionally they don't. It's hard.

In fact I have a lot of respect for all the international captains.

There were extensive celebrations in Antigua, culminating in a karaoke session in a casino. Next, we had seven one-dayers, which were the weirdest set of non-matches because we lost so much to the weather. The series finished 2–2 when we won the last game in Barbados but there was a huge bonus for us. Andrew Strauss had been selected and from the minute he arrived, he looked an England player. In everything he did, his preparation, training, the way he spoke, the way he acted in the dressing room. He had that calmness and I thought to myself: 'This guy's going to be pretty good.' With several batsmen reaching the end of their career, it was a huge relief to bring in a new player and straight away know we had a good one.

I had now reached a point in my captaincy when I was not only concentrating on what I was doing, but also what my opponents were up to – seeing if there were any tricks to be picked up by analysing why they were doing this, that or the other. I believe that a lot of the art of captaincy is to motivate your players into giving everything when they get out there, but the tactical side cannot be ignored. Part of it is having your gameplans: when to have two gullys for Lara, when to have two men back on the hook. But another vital part is knowing when to talk and what to say when you do, picking the right time for a hand on the shoulder or a boot up the arse. I was still trying to perfect that art during our stay in the Caribbean, although to be honest I had had very little to say apart from 'Well done'.

Breaking open the champagne with Andrew Strauss and Mark Butcher after England's victory over New Zealand in the Headingley Test, 2004.

Laid-back New Zealand skipper Stephen Fleming relaxes in the Long Room. He told me not to listen to talk about being too calm for the captaincy.

Flintoff pulls a ball for six during his career-best innings of 167 in the Second Test at Edgbaston against the West Indies.

Trescothick takes the attack to the West Indies. He became only the ninth Englishman to make 100 in each innings.

Middling it against West Indies at Lord's, 2004. Wicketkeeper Ridley Jacobs looks on in dismay as England forge on to win by 210 runs.

Above: Steaming in at around 96mph is West Indies' Fidel Edwards.

Right: Brian Lara smites us at Lord's 2004. I've always got on well with him.

Below: Graham Thorpe and I celebrate another ten-wicket victory over the Windies – this time at The Oval in 2004.

Flintoff highly amused in the Second Test against the West Indies at Edgbaston – he had skied a six into the stands where his own father put it down.

Right: A majestic Jacques Kallis helps put a stop to England's winning streak of ten Tests in Cape Town, 2005. South Africa beat us by 196 runs.

Below: Ntini flying past Trescothick in Johannesburg, 2005 – big scores, big win for England.

Nice shot for nowt – caught for 20 off Ntini in the Third Test, Cape Town, January 2005.

Kevin Pietersen smashes South Africa all over Goodyear Park, Bloemfontein, in the second one-day international, 2005. Mark Boucher registers hurt.

The Barmy Army make the lads feel right at home in Barbados.

A captain's responsibilities can be many and varied. Here I'm forcing Darren Gough to smile at Edgbaston in the 2005 NatWest Series.

Wherever the captain is, there's always a camera trained on him. It's almost as if they're trying to invade your soul…

8

IN THE PSYCHOLOGIST'S CHAIR:
Harmison, Flintoff, Vaughan

Steve Harmison went to the West Indies as a bowler capable of great deeds. He came back a star. People ask how that happened. Well, Steve's a huge talent: he's got such pace and bounce. It's no real effort for him, it's just a natural thing. The seed of talent is there and we've tried hard to provide the conditions in which it can thrive.

Travelling is always going to be a problem while he's playing for England because he hates being away from the people that he knows best. If we're playing in London, eight of his friends will come down from the north-east for every day. Some people in our country don't understand that, but some guys just don't like being away from their home environment.

His travel concerns are something we've had to manage, although his attitude has been great. We just try to keep him entertained. We don't send DVDs to his room or anything like that, but we try to make sure he doesn't have too much time to himself. Flintoff and Robert Key are big mates of his so I encourage the two of them to try to stay close to him, to stop his mind wandering. If he's in his room on his own he'll make dozens of calls a day back home, spend all day on the phone. We all have single rooms and in 2003 he had big problems sleeping while in Bangladesh, and in the West Indies he struggled a bit especially for the first week and a half.

Those first weeks are the loneliest because you aren't playing, just training. Training days are always long but playing days fly by. Steve finds it really tough so we try to keep people close to him.

You have to keep an eye on Steve and Freddie, but they have worked their knackers off and it's been no coincidence that they are getting the rewards. Basically, I think both of them are a little insecure. They like to be loved and have people believe that their ideas are the right ones. It gives them big confidence when you back what they are thinking.

I'd love to see both of them carry on for decades, but I am realistic enough to know it probably won't happen. Indeed, I'd be surprised if Steve plays past his 30th birthday. I think he will continue long enough to earn what he needs to keep himself and his family for the rest of his life. It won't be millions but I suspect he'll get to a level when he thinks: OK, that's enough for me. He'll have his house in Ashington and his mates down the working men's club. They love their sport up there so there will always be jobs for him.

As for Flintoff, people mention him as an outside candidate to be a future captain. But he bats, bowls and fields – I'm not so sure giving him the extra responsibility and all the other jobs that come with captaincy would be good for him. The workload would be overwhelming. He'd have to practise his batting, bowling and then half an hour in the slips and then think about the captaincy. That would be very tough.

If Freddie gets the opportunity, his life will have to change from how it is now. He likes his fun and games and so do I – but at the right time. He couldn't act as he's acting now and be captain. He might have simmered down in two or three years' time and he might be able to do it because he has a good enough cricket brain, but the key to the captaincy is managing other people.

I am always wary of people coming out and saying: I want to be captain. Players occasionally switch counties because they are desperate to do the job, but it doesn't often work out. When the captaincy is considered if you can prove you're good enough it will come to you. The people who are going to choose you, they have to see it in you.

I remember Trescothick writing an article in a cricket magazine about what kind of captain he'd like to be. I thought he was putting himself under a load of pressure. Alec Stewart did something similar after hearing the whispers that he should be the next captain, got the job and within 12 months he was sacked. This kind of speculation can affect a player, and other people's opinion of that player. If you get the job through the back door and walk in unnoticed it's a lot easier.

In 2002, before I became captain, our sports psychologist Steve Bull gave me a thought about looking in the mirror. It's a kind of poem, the most insightful piece of literature you'll ever read on this theme. I gave it to the players when I took over and told them that it explained everything that I'm about. I suppose the underlying message is that you have to be honest with yourself because if you aren't, you aren't going to be honest with others.

When I mentioned ideas along these lines to Freddie, I think it hit home. I've never had to act like a dictator. Cricket is a team game, but you look after yourself, particularly on a Tuesday and Wednesday before a match. If you feel it's right to go to the pub or bat for three hours in the nets, then that's what you do.

When we train, whatever time we start, I expect everybody to be there and in the correct gear. Then, whether it's for 15 minutes or three hours we just give it everything. After that the players can do whatever they want. I put as much emphasis as possible on the player looking after himself because I know what works for me, and everybody else should know what works for them. If I have two pints of Guinness or sleep in the afternoon or go to the cinema or play golf, that might be just right for me, but it's not necessarily the same for everybody. I tell them to manage their own lives and careers, to know exactly what's wrong with their own game and do something about it. Captain yourself on and off the field. I have taken that approach with Freddie and he has responded.

Giving players responsibility is important. I give all the squad the opportunity to speak and sometimes insist that they do so. If you are hearing just my voice and Duncan's all the time, it becomes too repetitive and boring. In team talks and meetings we try to involve the players as much as possible. It helps mature them. I think ahead about what I'm going to talk about in the huddle. I'll go to some players half an hour before and tell them it's their turn to speak and they'll protest: 'Oh no, I haven't got time.' I have to do it regularly. Giving people a taste of what it's like to be captain helps breed understanding of how hard the job is.

I don't have to speak out that much because I have a good set of lads who work hard. But before every single game I'm thinking: have we picked the right team, have I made the right change, what's the best field setting, but I've never once seriously thought I shouldn't have taken this job. I know we have had success, but it's still a real mind-draining role and people view you differently than before. It is also very time consuming and you don't really have any days off. Previously, if you had finished on the Sunday of a Test, you'd have a week off. Those perks have vanished now. You're constantly on the phone, discussing changes, decisions, positions, and talking to the media. Basically you're in the papers every day, with people giving their opinions about you. You've got to deal with those opinions from ex-players and writers, who are not just talking about you as a player, but also as a person, scrutinising your family life, every aspect. I didn't understand how complex a job it was.

When Nasser was occasionally grumpy, I often didn't understand why. Now I do. Maybe I haven't been grumpy, but I have certainly been uptight in the last year and a half because of the job.

It's bound to change you as a person. You are under more pressure and you have to think about matters of a professional kind all the time. There are pressures on your time, everybody wants a piece of you, you become much more visible and more susceptible to stress. There are times when you take that stress home with you. One thing I quickly realised was that when that happens, you have to do something about it very quickly or the relationships you hold dearest come under pressure. Whatever the effects of captaincy on me, I was determined it was not going to affect my home life adversely.

The batting side and the occasional lack of runs I could

cope with because every batsman goes through spells when the ball does not get off the square as often as he would like. Captaincy was harder. I'm pretty calm and laid back, but I do take the job very, very seriously.

I'm always trying to think about how we are going to improve and move to the next level; how am I going to get that little bit extra out of a player; when's the right time to talk to a player; when's the right time to give him a rollocking or encouragement; when's the right moment to get the team together to talk about an issue. All these things have to be considered very carefully because if you get your timings wrong then the suggestions you are giving become irrelevant. I do think about the team a lot.

For example, during the 2004 one-dayers, I was playing badly, the team was playing badly and Nichola probably got the brunt of it at home. Not in a nasty way, but I'd just sit there and not talk and didn't have either conversation or energy. It was purely because I was thinking about the team and how we could improve.

Nichola is very understanding and full of support, but I said to her that I was going to have to do something about the way I sometimes behaved. I wasn't happy about it, so that's when I started seeing our sports psychologist Steve Bull on a one-to-one basis. We worked on techniques so that once I was away from the ground, that was it; the events of the day were not clogging up my mind and taking over. It's impossible to blot things out completely and I still thought about the game, but I tried to relax more and get on with everyday life. I'm sure every captain in the world would say exactly the same, that you do take the job home. You have to do to some extent, but you've also got to be able to switch off and get away from it because if you don't you'll just go barmy.

Strangely enough, there is more pressure in the job when you're winning. Because we were winning all the time in the Tests, people thought it must be easy, but nothing could be further from the truth. With victory comes an increase in expectation levels. When you're losing, then expectations remain low. When you win then it is expected that you continue doing so and that your performance levels will stay high. Doing that is not as easy as it sounds.

I try to be as normal as I can with the players, but what I find is that when England win a game and you're the captain, people look at you in a completely different way. They think you are some kind of wizard with a magic formula. I'm not. I captain the team my way, but I'm still the same bloke, not something from Harry Potter. The stresses of the job cause different reactions in you, but I always try to be realistic and honest with myself and the team. I try to keep within the team boundaries and to make sure we work hard and prepare. The only time I come down on the players is when I think their attitude isn't right. If your attitude is spot on and you don't perform, then there's not a lot you can do, but if it's slightly off then there's plenty you can do.

You make mistakes in every game whether in batting or captaincy or something you might have said. Nobody's perfect and I know I'm not. It would be easy to hide and pretend that everything you do is correct. Even in winning, you make mistakes, but obviously I've done okay somewhere because we have won quite a lot of games. I must have said some things right, but I'm not one of these characters who thinks he is always right.

There are times when we've been in the field and I've said to Thorpe or Trescothick, 'Captain for an hour, will you? Don't do the directing bit, but come and tell me what you want done during this hour.' It gives me a break and increases their involvement and thinking. That's why I like others to speak in the huddle, because it's almost as if that session is theirs and they feel as if they have to lead the other players through it. Different voices give everybody a chance to develop a sense of responsibility and drive.

9

THE SUMMER OF SEVEN–LOVE:
New Zealand and West Indies 2004

The summer of 2004 would bring me into direct contact with Stephen Fleming, somebody I admire greatly and with whom I have shared a dressing room. Stephen's been captain of New Zealand for eight years and that says a lot about the man, his resilience, character and ability. To be captain for that length of time – and to do the job to the standard that he has – is nothing short of incredible because it drains you. One of the most impressive things over the last year or so is that his batting has improved after he had struggled for two or three years. When we played him in 2004 I could recognise a really good batsman. He didn't have that tag before because he was known as a pretty good player who could play the odd really good innings, but he lacked consistency. He had a few technical flaws, but 2004 saw a sound, technically correct batsman with a strong head. He has always been a good reader of one-day situations and a good judge of when to play the right innings. This year we also saw it in his Test game: he was a hard player to get out, knew his own game and had worked out a plan of how to play Test cricket. He had had real success in Sri Lanka the year before as a batsman and brought that over to England.

Fleming's style of captaincy has always been acknowledged throughout the world as one of the best. I was fortunate to play with him for Yorkshire when he had a short spell as our overseas player in 2003. The one thing you noticed was his presence in the dressing room and on the pitch. There was an automatic respect because of what he gives you back, despite his being a big name. He never looked down on any player no matter how young or old or good or bad. Yorkshire would have been more than happy to have him back and maybe they will in the future, although he went on to sign for Nottinghamshire for 2005.

Stephen certainly made his mark on the Yorkshire team. He didn't score that many runs, but his presence was immense. It wasn't so much his thought processes towards the game, but the respect he commanded. We were struggling because we lacked experience but once he arrived results started to change. He helped the young captain Matthew Wood both on and off the pitch.

I suppose his reputation was made when he took his young New Zealand side to Australia in 2001–02 and held them to a draw. Without a good attack and that one world-class player it's very difficult to set imaginative fields. But Fleming had Shane Bond. Once you had Bond bowling really well and fast he was allowed to set weird and imaginative fields, something I was fortunate to do later with the likes of Harmison and Flintoff. You have to have the bowlers to do that and he shook the Aussies up with his gameplan. He packed the gully regions with three and four fielders and invited players such as Gilchrist and Martyn to cut. He had a little bit of luck and the ball kept going to hand, but you create your own luck by innovating.

Fleming is very thoughtful and I am particularly impressed by how he goes about his job in such a calm manner. When I got the England job, I said I would do it my way, but my way was more a Fleming way than a Hussain way.

Fleming kept his cool in all situations. He never seemed to get flustered, wave his arms around, kick dirt, hurl his cap on the floor or show any noticeable emotion if players made mistakes. He just controlled everything in a measured fashion although he obviously had harsh words to say in the sanctuary of the dressing room. His team on the field always appeared to have a huge amount of respect for him.

When I went back to Yorkshire after one England game as captain, he sat me down and asked me how I was finding it. It was all new to me and I just said I was trying to learn as I went along, but that I couldn't believe the amount of criticism I was taking especially when people said I was too laid back, calm and casual for the job.

Fleming just said: 'Don't listen to that, it's a load of crap.' He said he had got it in the neck from Martin Crowe during his first 18 months in the job, with Crowe constantly in the media saying Stephen wasn't tough enough and didn't show enough emotion on the pitch. Fleming said to me that emotion doesn't win you games of cricket. He told me he liked the way I was dealing with things on the pitch, that my mannerisms were pretty similar to his and that he guessed that we were pretty similar people – laid back and playing the game as we saw it; trying to be as professional and thoughtful as we could, but realising it's not the be-all and end-all.

Just speaking to him for half an hour was very enlightening although I got few chances to play with him for Yorkshire. We did combine against Warwickshire in a day/night match and he got 139 not out. I got 30-odd and we won a good game. We had a decent partnership and he seemed very humble out in the middle. He was quite emotional about scoring a century for Yorkshire. That again told me the kind of person he was. He'd played hundreds of big games, but it really meant a lot to him to score a hundred for his new county because he actually respects the game and the traditions. He knew Yorkshire had a long history and he was adding to it by scoring that hundred. He spoke in the dressing room afterwards not only about how much he'd enjoyed his stay but also about the way he felt the club should go. It's clear to me that he thinks before he opens his mouth. He doesn't speak for the sake of it, but does so when things need to be said and when his words will do some good. He's also a very clever man.

When Fleming arrived at Yorkshire the club was in a really bad state. There was a new captain in Anthony McGrath, who then got into the Test team, so Matthew Wood took over. There were a lot of comings and goings and injuries, the influential Aussie Darren Lehmann wasn't there any more and one or two overseas players had come and not made much impression. We didn't have a coach either and Kevin Sharp had taken temporary control. Fleming was a breath of fresh air. He grabbed the dressing room straight away – helping the team knit together and gain a new focus and the results changed instantly. He wanted the players to look at themselves, be honest and really value the traditions of the club. I'm not one for going back into the past, but when there are histories and traditions you have to respect them.

Later in 2004, listening to him at the captains' meeting before the ICC Trophy competition, I thought we had a similar view about the game and we got on very well. I'd taken a few bats with me to get signed, there were six in all and I could see just how happy he was when I gave him one. He was really grateful that he had a bat with every captain's signature on it. It was another example of how much he respects the game.

New Zealand lacked the firepower of Bond on their 2004 visit, but Fleming didn't use that as an excuse. Instead he said that England, with Harmison bowling beautifully, were going to be a threat against anybody in the world. He would be the first to admit that once you have a world-class bowler it makes the captain's job a lot easier. They may have lacked that individual brilliance but New Zealand had a fantastic structured game, in the field and when batting. All the players knew their roles, fielding disciplines and drills. I'd faced them in New Zealand under Nasser and we drew 1–1 in a series we really should have won. I knew them to be a well-disciplined team with strong all-rounders in Chris Cairns, Scott Styris and Daniel Vettori.

We always felt the New Zealand series would be tougher than the Tests against West Indies later in the summer. By the time we arrived home from the Caribbean it was already six weeks into the season. Then I twisted my knee in practice, which forced me out of the First Test, so Trescothick was in charge as we began a run which would eventually lead us into the record books.

It was a twisted knee which turned into a twist of fate because it enabled Andrew Strauss to come in and establish himself as an opening batsman. New Zealand reached 386 in their first innings thanks to an impressive 93 from Mark Richardson, a couple of useful half-centuries from Nathan Astle and Jacob Oram, and a typically belligerent 82 from Cairns, who created carnage for an hour before Harmison caught him off Flintoff, which made a change from the usual c Flintoff b Harmison entry in the scorebooks.

Strauss strode out for his Test debut as if he had been in the team for a decade, scoring a glorious century and receiving a richly deserved ovation. We were able to accumulate a handy first-innings lead of 55.

Richardson had been denied a century in the first innings, but chiselled one second time around and we were left with a victory target of 282.

It looked a long way off when our first two wickets went down for 35, but Strauss showed that his first innings was not a fluke, but just an illustration of what was to come. He was robbed of another century by a run-out to leave centre stage to Hussain.

Nasser played for most of his century as he had throughout his career – dogged determination aligned to power and astuteness – but he reached it in Flintoff style, three successive boundaries taking him to a hundred and us to victory. Nasser decided soon afterwards that it could only be downhill after that and retired.

It saved us a selection headache because he would have had to play the next game and Strauss, despite his heroics, would have been dropped. But I think Nasser had seen a player who would be playing Test cricket for some time and he didn't want to get in the way by just playing an extra few games to get his 100 caps. Nasser rang me between Tests to say that he couldn't have wished for a more appropriate way to end his career and that he was calling it a day. I wished him well and congratulated him on an outstanding career.

The team would now have to move on without yet another senior player, having lost Atherton, Stewart, Caddick, Gough and now Hussain. The squad was going in its own direction with younger stock and new ideas. It's sad to see established players go, but it's also exciting knowing that a new era is starting. Nasser's sudden decision to quit prompted us to drop me down to No. 4 so that Strauss could continue opening. I didn't mind at all. Strauss looked comfortable there and we had spoken about it before so that we were ready when Nasser retired. I actually like the No. 4 position.

It was weird watching the match at home and not being there, but it had been a wonderful performance. Then it was off to Headingley which was always going to be a tricky week for me because Nichola was due to give birth. I was determined to be there when the baby arrived and I had permission to leave the ground if Nichola went into labour. The only time I would have stayed was if I was batting or just about to go in. I'd been told on the Friday morning that the waters had broken, but there was no panic because the likelihood was that it could be a while. I spoke to Duncan at tea when we were in the field and he said that the baby was obviously on its way so I should do an hour and then leave early to avoid getting stuck in traffic. Tallulah Grace was born at two minutes past nine and there was a bit of a media frenzy when I returned to the ground on Saturday morning.

New Zealand totalled 409 which at Headingley is too

many and then Trescothick led our reply. Flintoff made a thunderous 94 but Geraint Jones's innings, a debut Test hundred, was perhaps the most significant. He grabbed the match from New Zealand and repaid very quickly the faith we had placed in him.

New Zealand really missed Shane Bond and it could have been different had he been with them because they just didn't have the one guy who could bowl that special spell. We always knew what was coming at us. Our first-wicket partnership of 153 vindicated our decision to change the order. Hoggy and Harmy disintegrated their second innings and we needed just 45 to claim our second win and the series.

It was an extra special week for me both on and off the field – beating a really good Kiwi side and becoming a father for the first time.

With many of the old guard gone, England were moving in a direction where I could see us having basically the same squad for both Test and one-day matches. I see no reason at all why if you can perform in one form of the game, you can't in the other. I would never completely dismiss players specialising in just one division, but I was determined to have people who wanted to play in both forms.

Trent Bridge looked like somewhere New Zealand might find consolation when they reached 271 for two, but once again we fought back. The collapse that followed meant that we were able to restrict them to 384 when 500 had looked inevitable. The Kiwis were still favourites when they shot us out for 319 – a disappointing total.

Giles, who had been showing for some time that he had no peer as England's premier spinner, aided by the deadly Harmison and Flintoff, then whittled them out for 218, and our second innings started with us needing 284 for a white-wash. No one had ever won a Test at Trent Bridge chasing more than 247 in the fourth innings. Three of us were back in the pavilion before we had 50 on the board so it seemed we might be in for a jolt. It is at times like these that experience is vital. Thorpe's unbeaten hundred was one of the finest of his career and with Ash showing that he was becoming another all-rounder, we were able to get home in some style with four wickets in hand.

The match was over in four days which enabled us to watch the England v France match at the Euro 2004 football championships on the Sunday night. The celebrations over, it was then home for a week with the family as the Vaughan household had now become.

When it was back to business, it was for a one-day series involving New Zealand and West Indies. I was a little worried because we didn't quite have the structure I would have liked. We played very badly throughout, lost to both sides and never gave ourselves a chance of reaching the final, doubly disappointing in a home series. There was a lot of talk about my batting because the highest score I'd got was 14. I played badly and didn't feel like I was in any kind of form, but refused to be too hard on myself. We made wrong selections and that had to improve. On every occasion a team won the toss, bowled and then chased down the runs. The only toss we won, we won the game. It's no excuse, but in our conditions bowling first does make a big difference. We had to find a way of winning without winning the toss, because that's not guaranteed.

We were rightly criticised and I decided to take a few days off to work with Duncan. I batted for hours in the academy against a variety of bowlers with him studying my approach. My balance and weight distribution were out of synch and I just needed to groove things again. I left those sessions knowing I was in a better state of mind and better form. I went to Lord's and the First Test against West Indies ready because I was now hitting the ball in the areas I wanted to.

Freddie came back from an ankle problem towards the end of the one-dayers but was unable to bowl, so we went into the First Test not wanting to throw him the ball too much. Still, it was reassuring to know that, if needed, he was there.

We had now won seven of our last eight Tests. Lord's turned into a run-fest which was not what Lara had in mind when he invited us to bat, only to see the early clouds burn off. Strauss made his third century in as many internationals at Lord's, and Key drove his way to 221, owing his success to another kind of driver – the one who had rear-ended Butcher's car before the game, giving Mark whiplash and Key a call up to bat at No. 3. My hard work with Duncan paid off with a century, an instant reward which was very satisfying.

Despite a defiant century from the experienced Chanderpaul, West Indies fell 152 short of our total and we were able to push along our second innings at a rate. Lara just did not have a cutting edge among his bowlers and used seven in all, none of whom troubled me greatly and I marched on to a second century while Freddie ransacked 58 in next to no time to help us declare 477 ahead. That target always looked beyond them, though a draw did not, at least until Giles bowled Lara on the last morning. The ball dipped unexpectedly, spat through Lara's defence and clattered middle stump. Giles ended with nine wickets, which was a tribute to perseverance and dedication in the face of criticism, even ridicule. He's our best spinner by a long way.

Lord's was becoming a very happy ground for me. After that match, I had 13 Test hundreds and four of them had come at headquarters. It is a very satisfying feeling and psychologically helpful knowing that the ground on which you have been most successful is the one where you play the most, because we now play two Tests a year at Lord's.

In the dressing room afterwards I had a drink and a bit of a laugh with Brian Lara, chatting about the game and our common passion, golf. We even spoke on the phone to Ernie Els, winner of three golf majors.

Next was Edgbaston and after talking to the groundsman, I discovered that the wicket was particularly dry. Even just ten minutes before the toss, the covers were still on and there were no clouds. He was obviously a little worried that he'd got it too dry and wanted to keep as much moisture in it as he could. I knew the toss was vital and won it. Remarkable things were now happening in the side. Trescothick made a hundred in each innings, taking the attack to them. Before the start of this series the feat had been achieved only eight times by an Englishman; now it had happened two Tests in a row. And Freddie belted 167 which included a memorable six into the Ryder Stand. From a crowd of 20,000, Fred somehow picked out his dad – who dropped it. Even in their first innings the wicket was deteriorating and we set them a near-impossible 479. So it proved. We had played good cricket, but the toss had been crucial because I'd never seen an Edgbaston wicket like it: uneven bounce, very dusty and lots of cracks.

Flintoff was scoring 50s at will and the team was thriving.

We were 2–0 up going to Old Trafford, but first we cele-brated in Birmingham – there were quite a few celebrations in 2004 – and had a few days off, which gave some of us a chance to go back to our counties and play in the C&G quarter-finals. I managed to get Yorkshire 116 not out to win the game against Lancashire. I was delighted: I love going to play for Yorkshire because they are a good set. I always like to see England players going back to their coun-ties and giving as much for them as they do for the inter-national team and for me it's refreshing to go back and just be one of the lads rather than captain.

The Old Trafford Test wicket was quite a quick one and it suited Fidel Edwards, whose bowling was sharp. It should also have helped our pace men, but for the first time in a while we didn't bowl as well as we can in their first innings. The fields were a little too aggressive and we were bowling too short, and despite getting Lara for a rare duck, the West Indies still totalled 395. Our reply of 330 owed much to another Thorpe hundred, made despite a broken finger after Edwards hit him. It looked like we might be in for an uncom-fortable journey.

If our bowling had been wayward in the first innings, it was lethal in the second. Harmison, with four wickets, and Flintoff and Giles combined with some reckless batting to leave a victory target of 231.

We lost early wickets, but Key hit 93 – a match-winning innings which was actually better than his double-hundred at Lord's because it was compiled on a trickier wicket. We were now in the same position we had been in the Caribbean: three up after three and looking to apply the final gloss to a whitewash. This time we intended to do it.

By the time we arrived at The Oval, Lara's men were quite hurt and beaten up. If they lost the toss, it would be very difficult bordering on impossible for them. I won it and was more than happy to bat.

Despite us losing three wickets for 64, I managed to steady the ship somewhat, aided by the very impressive Ian Bell, looking a class act on his debut.

We shared a partnership of 146, helping us towards an acceptable total of 470. Between them, Lara's team-mates did not manage to equal the 79 he himself scored and I had no problem inviting them to bat again. It wasn't as easy second time round as Gayle made a smash-and-grab hundred, but when their last wicket fell at 318, we needed just one run. We had been confident of beating West Indies, but to win all seven Tests in a summer for the first time ever – equalling the record for successive England victories – was very, very special. The win also consolidated our rise to second in the world rankings – behind only Australia.

It was particularly encouraging to see Bell come into the team and do well straight away. It said to me he was graduating into an environment he was happy and comfortable with. It's important that young players feel at home and relaxed because it gives them the confidence to continue playing the way they have done to get into the side in the first place.

10

MEETING AND BEATING THE AUSSIES:
The ICC Champions Trophy 2004

The ICC Trophy, a kind of mini World Cup, played at home in September, was a timely competition for us to gauge how quickly we were developing as a one-day side. Flintoff was back bowling, Vikram Solanki returned and Alex Wharf, a thumping pace bowler from Glamorgan, was included for the first time. Trescothick and Solanki went in first, I dropped to No. 3, followed by Strauss, Flintoff, Collingwood, Jones as keeper, Giles, Wharf, Gough and Harmison at No. 11.

There was a much better feel about the one-day squad when we got together for a warm-up series against India. We hammered them at Trent Bridge, beat them convincingly at The Oval and lost the last one at Lord's when I managed to make 74. I'd made a couple of slight technical changes and was now playing well. Our first victory was chasing, the second batting first which gave us an enormous amount of confidence.

We knew if we continued the way we played against India, we could definitely go a long way, possibly all the way, in the Champions Trophy. The draw meant that if we got to the semi-final then Australia would, in all likelihood, be waiting.

Throughout the tournament I kept telling the players that this big prize was waiting for us when the tournament got down to its last four. We set our goals to ensure that we got there. We wanted to play the best and Australia were undoubtedly that.

Paul Collingwood, fast developing into one of the world's best one-day players and without peer in his fielding abilities, engineered an escape against Zimbabwe at Edgbaston with 80 not out after we had been reduced to 123 for four by an attack which could hardly be described as the best in the world. Colly has an acute cricket brain and can adapt to suit any situation. It was down to him that we reached 299 for seven, a target that was always going to be beyond Zimbabwe's grasp. They ended more than 150 short.

Sri Lanka were always going to be a trickier test at the Rose Bowl and we were indebted to a slow-burning hundred from Flintoff for our 251 for seven. The weather butted in, leaving Sri Lanka stranded, well behind the Duckworth/ Lewis required score on a grudging pitch. Now, instead of dark clouds on the horizon, the even more ominous presence of Australia loomed.

It was a match which, in some ways, we could not lose. Very few people outside the England dressing room gave us any chance. There was a real buzz going into the game although an article Harmison wrote in the *News of the World*, about not going on the forthcoming trip to Zimbabwe, created a bit of confusion. We tried to put it to the back of our minds.

Surprisingly, it wasn't a full house at Edgbaston, but the atmosphere was electric for a match between the best team in the world and one aspiring to that position. They scored quickly and all their top five batsmen got a start but none could take the game away from us. Only Damien Martyn with 65 and my former Yorkshire colleague Darren Lehmann with 38 caused us any real concern and surprise, surprise, I got rid of both with my occasional tweakers.

A target of 260 was always on once Trescothick and I shared a second-wicket partnership of 140 and when I left with 86 to my name, my best in one-day internationals, we were only 33 short with plenty of wickets and overs to spare. Strauss continued the good work and we won by six wickets.

To get two wickets and play a crucial innings in a team that had just beaten Australia convincingly was very satis-fying and it took us into a major one-day final for the first time in 12 years. It's always tough on the pitch against Australia, but they are good lads and we got on quite well, knowing most of them through county cricket. They all came and had a drink with us later that night.

The press got a little carried away and, when asked whether this meant we could now win the Ashes, so did I. 'Rubbish!' I replied. There was absolutely no relevance between a one-day win and the Ashes.

We knew Australia were still some way ahead of us, but we had beaten them well – and we hadn't done that in a long time. We went to the Walkabout, an Aussie bar, to celebrate gently rather than with the normal gusto, knowing that the final was still to come.

The Oval and a full house and the nation right behind us: what more could we want? A good day would have helped, but the weather was dicey, overcast and drizzly all day. We just played through it, none more impressively than Trescothick, who scored an incredible century as seven different partners came and went at the other end.

I thought our 217 would be a winning total particularly as we chipped away at their batting almost from the off. When Lara was fourth out, with only 72 on the board and the pitch still lively, our chances looked extremely healthy. When we prised out the dangerous Chanderpaul with the total 147, with only two wickets remaining, the Trophy looked secure.

But two Bs turned into A-stars for West Indies. Courtney Browne was plum lbw first ball to Flintoff but given not out, and he and Ian Bradshaw then shared one of the finest one-day partnerships of all time given the circumstances. There was never a feeling that we would lose the game, but the way Browne and Bradshaw played was unbelievable. Harmison was bowling 92mph in the dark and two tailenders still stuck it out. Sometimes you can only hold your hands up and say well played. We didn't do much wrong.

Seeing Brian Lara collect the trophy ranked as one of the low points in my career, but I also had to be realistic. Knowing that we had reached a one-day final having been played off the park by both New Zealand and West Indies in the NatWest series meant there should not be too much self-criticism. We had come a long way and that's why I got all the team together in a huddle and said: 'I know we have just lost, but don't be too down on yourselves because we have made up a lot of ground in the last few weeks. Keep your chins up because you've had a fantastic summer. Be proud of yourselves.' It was still very quiet in the dressing room as I considered what had just happened. Perhaps it was fate. The West Indies had been torn apart by hurricanes Ivan and Jeanne and maybe this was somebody's way of lifting their spirits. It was almost destined that they were going to win.

11

A BLOODY MESS:
Zimbabwe 2004–05

Throughout the summer there always loomed the issue of the Zimbabwe tour, scheduled for the autumn, and whether we would go there. As soon as the indication came from our board that we would travel, I felt that we should take the best team.

That was our intention, a side picked on merit, but then we came into the Champions Trophy and played Zimbabwe. As soon as the match finished and we'd seen just how weakened they had become because of the defections and political wranglings, Fletch came up to me and said we might have to change our thinking and rest players. They were so feeble that playing five games in a week out there, against basically an academy team, wasn't going to do us any good. It was decided that some players might be just as well off having a couple of extra weeks' rest. We decided to take that course with our feeling being that it would be a good idea to rest five senior players including myself, so that we would be well prepared for the South Africa leg of the tour.

As soon as I saw the kind of team Zimbabwe had then I knew it was not the best plan to take a top side out there involving players who had played almost non-stop for five years home and away. An extra two weeks off was exactly what they needed and we felt our administrators should go along with it. If the coach thinks his players need a rest then they should rest.

The indications coming back from the board were that some of the others could rest, but not me. I could see their point. They wanted a senior guy, most obviously the captain, for what could be a tricky tour. My feelings were that, cricket-wise, the tour was so irrelevant and so likely to do us more damage than good that they should rest as many as possible. There would be senior officials from the ECB there anyway if there were any difficult situations developing.

Meetings and phone calls followed meetings and phone calls, the majority involving David Morgan, the ECB chairman. Meanwhile the chairman of selectors, David Graveney, was fully behind us. He wanted to do exactly the same, but Morgan overruled the selectors. He just said: 'Vaughan has to go, it's more than a cricket tour.' As soon as I heard that I started wondering: if it was more than a cricket tour, what the hell were we actually going there for?

I knew my body was knackered and needed rest and that if I and others were allowed extra time off we would have a better chance of beating South Africa – something I felt was very important to do. The Aussies and the Ashes were already on the horizon and I was anxious that every potential member of the squad was in the best possible condition for what was going to be the ultimate test for all of us.

I didn't think there could be a better way of judging just how good a team we were developing into than by seeing how we performed both individually and as a unit in South Africa. The more rested we were, the better our chances, I felt, because it was going to be a long, tough tour, demanding of both mind and body. It was also exactly what we needed with the Aussies only eight months away. If we did not perform well against one of the best sides in the world then our chances would be limited against *the* best.

I'm not 100 per cent sure what was going on behind the scenes or what pressure was being exerted from outside, but it became obvious that I would have to go.

Politics and sport don't mix for me, but there was absolutely no use getting too upset about it because I had enough on my plate and did not want to waste any unnecessary energy pacing up and down about something over which I had no control. In hindsight, it was probably the right decision anyway even if I might not have felt so at the time.

This time the situation changed because it was very clear there would be a huge financial penalty if we didn't travel, with a chance we could be banned for six months. If that happened it could crucify our game. It was decided that the tour had to take place.

I would rather we had not gone at all, principally because I think it's a disgrace the way Zimbabwe have got rid of many of their best players and now field a team which I do not feel comes up to international standard. It would if they fielded their best players, but they chose not to, although that situation would change some time later.

I thought it disappointing that the government were saying we shouldn't go. If they didn't think we should be going then they should just have pulled us out and said that whatever financial implications there were, they'd deal with them. There are only two ways you can get out of a tour: one is if your government pulls you out and the other is if there are safety and security issues. Then when I saw Jack Straw shaking Robert Mugabe's hand, however unintentional it might have been, I thought, we're going. They won't be shaking his hand one minute and then saying we shouldn't go the next.

I wasn't actually blackmailed into going, but I was pressured. The rest would have been welcome, especially after playing just about every game over the last four years, and I was disappointed after the success we had had that eventually our views counted for little. The whole situation was a bloody mess.

I got a call to say that Trescothick, Giles, Harmison and Flintoff would be rested. I said I'd go to Zimbabwe as long as that happened. I wanted them rested. I then got a call, when it was known that I had a suspect knee which might need a bit of a clean up, when the chairman tells me that if I don't go Trescothick will be captain. They were going to announce that he was to be rested, but would change that if I had to pull out. Then we were told Giles wanted to travel, wanted to support the team and didn't want to give up his position to anyone else. It showed a huge amount of character because he could easily have had two extra weeks at home with his wife and two kids. So they told me not to worry because if I didn't go then Giles would be captain. My head was going round in circles.

An easy decision had become a very complicated one. I got to the stage where I really did not need the hassle! It was our wedding anniversary and there I was, walking round the Chatsworth estate in Derbyshire with my wife and baby girl, taking calls from here, there and everywhere and I just said to Nichola in utter frustration: 'What the hell is going on?'

I'd never give up my position because I love the job, but this was the first time I had ever felt inclined to do so and it was not a nice experience. I spoke to Graveney an hour or two later and told him that I didn't need the pressure and that I could quite easily just go back to trying to get into the team as a batsman only. I didn't need those phone calls all the time. A couple of hours later I was fine, but for an hour or so I was on the point of wondering if it was all worthwhile.

Duncan fought on the resting issue and once he gets a view, he doesn't budge. I'd had a couple of meetings, he'd had about ten, and he knew just how important rest was. He knew it was going to be politically tough, but he was adamant.

He rang me up and told me to make myself available and if I then had to pull out injured, I could. I knew how many meetings he had been at and how hard he fought just to get the four guys rested, so when he asked me it was an easy decision for me. Harmison had pulled out and Freddie said afterwards that he would have done so anyway if they hadn't said they were resting him. I had always had a feeling Harmison and Flintoff would pull out and I had every intention of backing whatever decision they took. Every player has the right to make his own mind up but the captain's is a different position. A player pulls out and somebody else comes in, but for a captain, it would be a huge issue. But as soon as my employers gave me no option, I had to agree to go. If I'd pulled out there would have been a massive effect on the team and we could have had eight or nine pulling out. I had to bite my lip because somebody had to front up. The easy option would have been to pull out, but as captain I felt I had a duty to go. I didn't want another person coming new into the job having to captain England in difficult circumstances.

The overall cricket situation that I inherited was similar to England's during their preparation for the Rugby World Cup. For the last 18 months of the build up, their coach Woodward was given everything he wanted. The Ashes is our equivalent so whatever we wanted, within reason, I thought we should have been given to afford us the best possible chance of beating the Aussies.

The board came round to my view and we now have our masseuse, eye specialist, and different fielding coaches etc. We have finally got everything covered and I still think that whatever the coach and captain want they should get. Do you suppose that if Alex Ferguson went to his board and said: I'm resting Rooney, Giggs and van Nistelrooy for three weeks because I want them fresh for the Champion's League, they'd turn round and say: No you're not; Rooney plays. Would they hell!

I knew about Harmison and Flintoff's intentions regarding Zimbabwe, but I'd been hoping that in the interests of the team and the family we were becoming, they might change their minds and join us. I was hoping in my heart we would remain a team and would travel together.

Freddie gave me an indication weeks in advance that he didn't think his conscience would allow him to go, but Steve hadn't said a word. In the two meetings we had had on the issue, when Morgan, John Carr of the ECB and Fletch spoke to us, Steve had never even raised the subject. If he was that concerned you'd have thought he'd have spoken out, but not a word.

He had signed to do columns for the *News of the World*

and it looked like he'd be doing an exclusive on the issue. It wasn't a bad story if that was his plan, but he didn't tell us until during the Champions Trophy when he asked to see myself and Fletcher and said he didn't think he could travel. The situation in Zimbabwe hadn't changed in 18 months since the World Cup and he didn't want to go.

We said that's fine, it's your decision, but we were hoping we would be able to rest you anyway, so you don't really need to make any comment in the press. Just hold fire. Steve didn't say anything. He was almost a gibbering wreck while trying to tell us he wasn't going so we thought something must have been happening. His story appeared in the *News of the World* the following day. He tried to get it taken out, but failed.

The actual tour was nothing like a normal one and we didn't want it to appear as one so we prepared by going to Namibia first. But as soon as we were about to fly to Harare we had to make camp in Johannesburg when the ECB dragged us off the flight because Zimbabwe had refused visas to 13 of the British press corps.

We seemed to have an unlikely ally in the ICC who were now dropping hints that we might be able to cancel the tour without penalty and that they were sympathetic to our cause because of the way the issue had been dealt with by the Zimbabwean government.

Eventually the visas were granted, a new four-match series (rather than five) was scheduled and we finally landed in Harare. Once there, we encountered very few problems and little, other than a few anti-Tony Blair posters, to suggest that people were anything other than mildly interested in our presence.

I just wanted to play the games, but I was definite about one thing – we'd quit the tour if we were forced to meet President Robert Mugabe. The ECB stressed that if there were any attempts to use us as political pawns then we would be free to quit. My sympathies went to the likes of Ian Bell, Matt Prior and Kevin Pietersen, who were on a senior tour for the first time. They were seeing things and being involved in meetings that they should not have been subjected to.

It quickly became obvious that Zimbabwe were still not the force they once were. The defections and political shenanigans had seriously depleted their playing resources and they were not anything like a match for us. They were all out for 195 in the first game, and we knocked them off for the loss of five wickets.

The second match in Harare was a little more competitive until Pietersen showed his strength and Geraint Jones his guile in lifting us to 263 for six. Pietersen's 77 not out was a foretaste of the savagery he would later inflict on his native South Africa. Of equal interest to me in this match was the bowling performance of Collingwood. It may have been second-class opposition, but he took three for 16 in ten overs at a time when we were hoping a fifth bowler, capable of bowling his maximum allocation without conceding too many runs, would emerge.

What surprised me after Pietersen's fine innings was when Angus Fraser, who played plenty of Test cricket himself and now writes for *The Independent*, came up to me and said: 'Who's going to have to open now, Straussy or you, now that Pietersen's in at three or four?' I found it bizarre that, just because Kevin hit 77 against a very average attack, our press was even thinking about moving either myself or

Strauss to accommodate him. He's definitely a good player, but a bit behind what Strauss and I had done at that time. When I said: 'Why can't he bat seven?', Fraser said: 'What?' He didn't seem to grasp that in today's one-day cricket your top nine, not just the top six, have to be able to bat to a very high standard. Everybody says the top six is where the runs come from, but that's absolute nonsense. One-day cricket now is about the pressure times and when Nos. 5–9 are in, you almost need your best players there. I couldn't believe where Gus was coming from and told him that I thought he was still playing in the 1980s when things were different.

Fletcher and I had often thought that we were always a middle-order batsman short, but in Zimbabwe I got the impression we might just have found him. Time would tell. Someone in those positions has to be able to clear the ropes and Kevin can certainly do that. We were hoping that he was more than just a banger because if we could get him in when the ball was old, say from 25 overs on, then he could be very dangerous indeed because he also hits spinners well. It was a feeling which would be confirmed soon enough and I was convinced that we were getting close to being a very, very good team.

The third match was basically another walkover as our opponents made just 238 and we knocked them off with just two down. It was in the final match particularly that Gough showed just how valuable he can be in this form of the game. After 90 from myself and 80 from Geraint gave Zimbabwe 262 to chase, Goughy ripped out their best batsmen and we completed a 4–0 clean sweep. But the series was far from satisfying.

12

ALL'S WELL THAT ENDS WELL:
South Africa 2004–05

We were happy to get out of Zimbabwe and get on with what we considered the proper part of the winter. Flintoff, Harmison, Thorpe, Key and Trescothick, fresh from the extra rest I envied them, arrived to augment the Test side. Strangely enough, and it was the first time I had encountered it, there was a peculiar atmosphere in the camp. I'd be lying if I said it wasn't a worry because although I couldn't exactly put my finger on it, I felt that there was a certain amount of spirit lacking. This was very unusual.

I couldn't nail it down: whether it was individuals worrying about their own game and starting to feel the heat knowing that we faced Australia next summer, or the Zimbabwe issue and resentment of the players who hadn't gone there. But I knew if it wasn't addressed then it could lead to something unpleasant. There was definitely something missing at the start of a Test series which I felt we had to win in order to send out the right message ahead of the Ashes.

I was 12th man in the one-day game against Nicky Oppenheimer's XI and it was obvious as I watched from the balcony that there was an attitude problem. I aired my concerns to Fletcher, but he wasn't sure what it was either. We decided to give the team the benefit of the doubt because this was only the start of the tour and to watch how things developed in the next warm-up match against South Africa A.

Again, we were miles short of where we wanted to be. The actual performance was not such a concern, it was the attitude. Something was wrong. Had we not set down our tour goals early enough? Maybe it was just a lack of form. But this was the first – and only serious – match before the Test series so it was hardly ideal preparation. I wasn't sure what to say or do, but I did know during the hammering we took that we had problems.

I spoke to each player individually in our hotel in Potchefstroom and told them that whatever was on their minds, whatever their worries and concerns, as soon as they left this room, they must put them all behind them and we must all get back to being the England team we had been three months ago. I told them that if they did so our attitude would improve, our work ethic would improve, and we would get the spirit back.

I thought that as soon as the Test matches started, the trouble would disappear. It didn't. But as we arrived for the First Test I also knew that if we had problems we were not alone. The South Africans had as many if not more. For some reason, believed to be political, Mark Boucher, their experienced wicketkeeper, would not be playing and injury kept out their key opener Herschelle Gibbs. We knew they had weaknesses, but the emphasis in the media seemed to be on our lack of preparation and not on the difficulties within the South African camp. We were denounced as being under-prepared and over-confident. There was so much anti-English talk and perhaps it got through to the players because the team showed some character. The South African media helped us enormously. They wasted no opportunity to criticise the way we played, particularly the TV commentators. We used it as a motivation, to try to prove them wrong all the time. They were driving us on, we responded to every barb and thanked them for it. We had to dig deep mentally and to come out of that Port Elizabeth Test with a win was pretty special.

We got Graeme Smith out first over of the series to give us a great start and put him under pressure. We knew he was a good player who had scored big against us previously so we wanted to nail him early and we did. It was a telling moment as Hoggard started the series the way he was going to continue, dominating with the ball. He showed good control, plenty of swing and a huge amount of heart throughout the series.

On that first day, in the windiest conditions I had ever encountered, our pace attack had great difficulty bowling into a gale blowing straight down the ground so we were forced to bowl Ash from that end after lunch.

At the end of the day he had sent down something like 24 overs for 40 runs. He controlled one end which allowed us to bowl the seamers downwind. They were 273 for seven at the close, which on a flat Port Elizabeth wicket, bearing in mind the wind and that we had only been able to attack from one end, was a great effort. All the commentators could say was what an opportunity we had wasted. Why didn't we attack them all day?

Strauss played almost flawlessly when we batted which was just as well because most of the rest of us contributed little. We should have had a massive lead, but we had to make do with 88, half what it should have been. We allowed them a foothold in the game and this would become a recurring theme throughout the series. One minute we would be dominant and then we would give them the initiative back – and so on. That was why the tour proved so mentally draining. Every single session ebbed and flowed and nobody could tell which way it was going to go.

South Africa are a very tough team to play against, particularly at home, and with a batting order as deep as any in the world. Nicky Boje often comes in at No. 9 and he has first-class centuries behind him so getting them out twice is never easy. Thankfully they misfired in the second innings as our bowlers, particularly Simon Jones who also removed Graeme Smith with the catch of the series, restricted them to 229 leaving a chase of 142. We were three down for 50, but Strauss was unstoppable and saw us home comfortably.

But that was the only thing which was comfortable. There remained an undercurrent of disunity. Even after the win things did not improve much. Maybe I was being too critical or sensitive and was seeing things that didn't exist. There was tension between certain players and management. There seemed to be conflict where previously there had been none. I asked Graham Thorpe, our senior player, to talk to the squad after our next practice session. He told them that whatever their motivation – money, family, pride, statistics – to call on it now for the benefit of the team. He did it very well indeed and his words briefly seemed to lift everybody. However, my concern about our general attitude nagged away going to Durban where we knew we would have to be at our best. We were anything but in the first innings, and were knocked over for 139. It was hot and humid and I had flu symptoms so I was itching to win the toss so we could bowl, which would have given me an opportunity to have half-hour breaks off the pitch. But we had to bat and I was in quite quickly and feeling dreadful – with shivering, headaches and sickness – although I didn't want to let them know.

Early inroads by our attack prompted the suspicion that there might be more in the pitch than had seemed likely, but as soon as we thought we might get back into the match the inimitable Jacques Kallis strode to the crease. The wicket was still doing a bit, but he made it look easy and thumped us to all parts to take his team to a first-innings lead of 193.

Before the series there had been a lot of talk about the South Africans being aggressive and coming after us verbally whenever possible. The game against their A side had been quite verbal so we went into the series expecting a barrage of abuse. There wasn't any. We thought they'd come at us from all angles with all kinds of rubbish, but it didn't arrive, at least until much later in the tour.

Now, with a lead of nearly 200, they still weren't as aggressive as expected. Strauss and Trescothick then put on a magnificent partnership of 273 which put us back in the game. Thorpe reached a hundred, and with Flintoff and Geraint Jones hitting a late flurry of runs, I was afforded the luxury of declaring on 570 for seven, a lead of 377. I am convinced we would have won and gone 2–0 up but for bad light cutting short the final session. But to get the initiative back was enormous for us. They had failed to seize the moment for although our two openers were superb, we had been sitting on the balcony expecting them to come at us hard and they didn't. Kallis's innings were arguably the best played against this England team and they should have nailed the game with such a big lead, but we finished on top. I think the series was won and lost in that game.

Still, to have got so close to winning was mentally draining. Not to do so definitely had a knock-on effect going into Cape Town where our unbeaten run came to a shuddering halt. We should have won our ninth Test on the trot, but hadn't and sometimes when that happens there is a psychological effect: when Arsenal's 49-match unbeaten run came to an end in 2004, they were in a state of confusion for a while. I was worried the same might happen to us.

I was beginning to get a reputation as a perennial toss loser and it was reinforced in Cape Town, where the wicket is always good to bat on for the first couple of days. Once again we found ourselves in the field and they played negatively, but I think they realised they needed 400 to put us under pressure. They got 441. We were drained and didn't have much resolve when we went out to bat so there were a lot of weak dismissals. We had taken a big knock in Durban and it was still being felt. We just didn't think well enough and 163 all out was miserable. South Africa took not the slightest chance second time round and waited until we needed more than 500 before declaring. We were tired and even though we took it to within 40 overs of a draw, defeat was not so much of a surprise to me.

There was a chink of light, however. Having bowled us out cheaply in the first innings, I was very surprised when Smith did not ask us to bat again. That gave me an indication that the South Africans were very wary of us. It gave us a confidence boost going to Johannesburg knowing that although we had lost it had only been by 40 overs. They could have thrashed us had they put us back in when sitting on a huge lead. Even when they started their second innings they did not bat aggressively and used up a lot of time. One great partnership and we'd have drawn. We were far from downhearted. We didn't get a fifty in the match which on a flat wicket had been a travesty. We sat down afterwards and told ourselves that it was impossible for us to play any worse and yet we still came close to a draw.

I had not batted well throughout the series and rather than have the scheduled few days off, I decided to go back into the nets with Fletcher. I wanted as much practice on my own as possible. I also wanted a team meeting before we left for Johannesburg because I had to clear the air on every issue. I knew a performance like the one at Cape Town had been coming. Some things were still not right and I told the squad that I had been worried all tour and if we didn't do something we were going to end up losing the series.

The meeting was crucial. I said that whatever had happened about Zimbabwe – and this was pointed at management as well – if anybody was holding any grudges or taking it out on those who didn't go to Zimbabwe, it had to stop now. That was done, finished, through. It was a load of manure we'd climbed out of and moved on from. I think that meeting was the reason we came back as hard as we did in the last two Tests.

The positive intensity in practice we had asked for was outstanding after that and there was a better buzz around the dressing room, more of the banter which had been lacking, and players were starting to enjoy one another's company again. You get to a stage when you are on tour so long that you can get fed up with people or voices. At the

Wanderers that England dressing room I had known was back. There was plenty of joking, people were helping one another and there was general and animated talking about the match. I felt a strong performance coming, from the team and myself.

Johannesburg was the best game we had played for a long time. To go in at 1–1 put us under a great deal of pressure, but we responded, not least Strauss who made another century. Although we gave them a couple of late wickets, we were 263 for four at the end of the first day. The next morning it was drizzling and dark, and the ball started swinging and seaming, reminding me of my debut there in 1999. I had to dig in because I hadn't got many runs and I wanted to bat as long as I could.

The light was an issue and I knew if the clouds were again around the following morning then we were going to have to take the opportunity to declare and bowl, in an effort to get the best of the conditions. I did just that, denying myself a probable hundred in the process, to try to get them under pressure. Within 20 minutes the sun popped its head from behind the clouds and stayed out all day. We didn't bowl well and lost Harmison with a little niggle. They ended up with an eight-run lead thanks to a century by Gibbs who, with Kallis, was a constant threat to our supremacy. I had been hoping we'd be ahead by 100. We dropped a few chances and they made the most of their luck. I knew we had to be positive when we batted again, that it was no use being tentative because we could find ourselves 50 for three or four and before we knew it we'd be in real bother.

I told the boys to take the game to them, to be positive without being reckless. Trescothick did just that, Strauss got out early for a change and Key fell after a quick 19. I arrived and together with my old opening partner I just went for it to put them on the back foot. It certainly worked because before we knew it they had scouts out in the field and were operating very defensively. We were allowed to milk runs.

We went into the last day knowing that anything could happen. We were 189 ahead with four down so if we lost quick wickets they would have been chasing around 250 on a pretty good track. Trescothick took away whatever hopes South Africa had with a typically unselfish knock. He smashed it so hard and fast that we were able to declare before lunch, leaving them an improbable target of 325.

Commentators felt we had left it too late to declare, but there was a reason I gave us just 68 overs to bowl them out. I just wasn't sure what I was going to get out of my seam attack. Hoggy was struggling with a hamstring strain and Flintoff was sore. I just didn't know what Harmison would produce and Jimmy Anderson, who had come in for Simon Jones because we thought it would swing, had not found his rhythm at all. So I couldn't really declare any sooner. We could have gone out and had no properly functioning seamers at all.

I wanted to give our bowlers a situation where South Africa couldn't really win the game and we could go out and attack with six slips all afternoon and see where it took us. Little did I know that Hoggard would bowl better than he had ever done in his life at this or any other level. He was incredible, taking seven for 61.

When you put a team under pressure on the last day, you know anything can happen. It did. Smith didn't come out to open because he had been concussed by a blow to the head in the nets; against doctor's advice he came in late in the innings, and tried to smash us everywhere – a strange tactic for a side trying to save a match. With them playing shots it gave us a chance. Maybe they thought they could get the runs. It was fine by us.

The victory was the best under my captaincy and of all the time I have played for England. To bowl out a South African team with nine batsmen on that last day was a very special, sweet moment. We were 2–1 up going into the last match. We also knew that given the weather at this time of year in Pretoria, it was unlikely that we would get five full days.

The victory was special for another reason too. On the second day, we started at 12 o'clock when it was dark and drizzling, Flintoff got out when it was pouring down and the umpires never came off the field. At the end of the day, when we were smashing it around in the dark, they came off. The South African fielders said they never appealed against the light. That wasn't the way I saw it because their wicketkeeper Boucher was holding up his arms and shrugging his shoulders to umpire Steve Bucknor at square leg.

I went into the media conference and said that all we asked for when interpreting the bad-light regulations was consistency from umpires and that we felt we hadn't seen it that day. I never even thought that I might be saying something I shouldn't; I was just trying to be honest. After being asked if the South African team had appealed, I just said in their position I'd have done exactly the same. We wouldn't have wanted to be on the pitch being walloped all over, which was exactly what was happening to them.

The next day I was told that I was being docked my £6,000 match fee and that the referee Clive Lloyd and the two umpires wanted to see me. I went in, they were there, but nothing happened and nobody said anything. When I asked why, they just said they were waiting for Graeme Smith. I couldn't understand what on earth it had to do with him or why he should be called as a witness for the umpires against me. I asked what he was a witness for and they said it was to disprove my comments about the South Africans asking for the light. I said: 'Well he did appeal,' while Smith claimed he didn't, adding that all he'd said was that his outfielders were struggling to pick up the ball. If that wasn't an appeal against the light, an appeal they were entitled to, then I'm not sure what is, short of just trooping off the pitch. The feeling in our camp was that the South Africans wanted me to get a ban and that's why Smith had gone in there. Whatever the situation, I know that I would never ever put myself in a position where I would be acting as witness against an opposing captain.

I felt my comments were justified and that I had not said anything out of the ordinary. I hadn't criticised Smith or his team because in their position I'd have wanted to come off as well. I just said that the umpires had been inconsistent on that second day. I lost my whole match fee and from that moment on, my relationship with Smith became very frosty.

I do respect him as a player because he's a good batsman and doing a good job as captain in difficult and often politically charged circumstances, but when I see him doing things like that then a loss of respect is inevitable. Whether or not he got sent in by their coach I'm not too sure. But I just call him 'The Witness' now and I don't think he likes it.

Our press guys thought it was ridiculous and I think we had sympathetic support from around the world in our appeal against the ruling. The ICC says there is no right of appeal for that type of offence, but we are going to take this as far as we can. That huge fine for saying what I did was in my opinion over the top. When you think of some of the things that do go on out there, it was very harsh.

The entire episode was quite sad really and I just did not understand Clive Lloyd's later comments about my being rude and dismissive. Anybody who knows me and my attitude towards people will tell you that that is not the case.

Things like that definitely drive a team on and it gave us an edge for the rest of the match. Victory was all the sweeter. We were determined to prove people wrong and to stuff South Africa out of sight. Our attitude never changed until our mission was accomplished. The unity and intensity in our play was back and throughout that last day I just sensed that something would happen. That was the difference between the sides, the way we played that afternoon. I was immensely proud of my team and gratified that the hard work we had all put in over a long period was showing such brilliant results.

Hoggard was the hero. He is a bowler who just keeps going for you, a reliable lad who will bowl 40 overs a day if you want him to. He doesn't always attack, but he keeps running in and he's very good fun on the pitch, although he does get nervous. I just try to relax him. In the first innings he got five wickets in conditions which were probably easier for him than in the second, when he took seven. If he'd bowled in the first like he did in the second, we'd have won in three and a half days.

What we had done throughout the series was to take every opportunity to put them under pressure whereas I felt it was always a safety-first approach by the South Africans. Fletcher was extremely pleased for us and I was delighted for him. Our relationship is crucial because we have to be very close and bounce ideas off one another. We might not always agree, but once we are in a team situation we both know the importance of singing from the same hymn sheet.

Duncan's a very clever thinker, easy to work with, and nothing less than brilliant technically. But it's weird: with our bowling attack you're never quite sure how they will perform and it's not always easy to gauge what to do, but I'm something of a gambler and in our first innings I wanted to give us the best chance of making use of the conditions. The declaration backfired on me a little because the sun came out, but I had no control over that.

On the last day I think some of the players would have preferred us to have batted on after lunch, to kill the game completely. That's not my approach. If an opportunity is there I want us to have a chance of taking it. If there's a chance to win, go for it because in the next game you may never get one. I think in the few years I have been playing, England have missed those chances to win games. That's why we did it.

We went to Centurion and when we got to the ground I realised they had created a result pitch, understandably in the circumstances of their being one down with one to play. There was plenty of grass and a few cracks so it was going to be a tough game.

The first day was washed out, the second saw 75 overs, the third 46. The weather was on our side, but I still think if we had played over the full five days, South Africa would not have beaten us. We would have played in a more attacking fashion. Once you lose so much time and they're still batting on day three then all you have to do is keep them out there for as long as possible. We eked out a lead of 112 and from that moment the series was won. We had them at 29 for two and if we'd got Kallis and A. B. de Villiers out quickly we would definitely have gone for the win. But those two both scored centuries at a fairly sedate pace, which ran the clock down.

I thought they might have given us 60 overs to get 160 or so, but they stayed out there batting, which was fine by us, and left themselves just 44 overs to get us out. They always seem to want to make sure you can't win before they think about doing it themselves. As it turned out we had a bit of a fright when three wickets went with more than 30 overs still to bat out. It left Thorpe and myself to count down the balls. It was typical that we really had to grind it out and fight because this had been the closest and toughest Test series I had been involved in for a long time.

Five Tests in six weeks is hard enough in itself, but every match went to the fifth day. It is very draining when you have no real breaks between games. Even the three days off we'd had in Cape Town, I'd spent in the nets. There had been more ups and downs than in a window-cleaning competition, quite a few of us were struggling for form and I was never quite sure what was going to happen when our bowlers came running in. It was also tough because for much of the series we hadn't been properly together as a team. That had worried me.

The expectation levels of some players were starting to affect them because they realised a lot of pressure was on them to perform, such were the standards they had set for themselves. It was getting to them and they were not performing as they had before.

In the final Test, we had also had to face up to the recalled fast bowler Andre Nel. He really does get in your face when you're batting and it rubs some people up the wrong way, but I don't mind him at all. He came in and bowled well. People just talk about his aggression, but he got the ball in the right areas and bowled good deliveries. Sometimes guys like that take a lot of wickets because batsmen try to smack them about because they're fed up. He actually bowled us out, though I don't think he got anybody trying to whack him. That was a sign of a decent bowler.

I like that kind of character. I'm all for people having a go with a few comments. I'd actually expected more, but it wasn't until too late that they started coming at us. It was do or die for them in that last game and Smith came out mouthing off and abusing players. As soon as we got to the crease he got stuck into us. It's fine, I didn't really mind it, but if you are going to do it, do it all the time. I certainly got stuck into him on the last day because I wanted him to know that we thought he'd treated some of his own players badly, never mind ours. We just wanted him to know a few things.

What astounded me was that he kept on calling me queer which I found very odd and childish. It was a schoolboy mentality, the kind of thing you'd say in the playground. He also kept calling Flintoff a big baby which I felt was very courageous, but also remarkably silly.

The stupid thing was that with Andrew Hall and Nel you have naturally aggressive players and I think if they had played in the Second Test at Durban, and shown that kind of spirit, then they could easily have won instead of being saved from losing by bad light. I am sure Smith regrets that.

To be fair to Smith, he came up and apologised for what he had been saying on the pitch when we bumped into one another in the hotel bar later that evening. I just said, 'Don't worry about it, mate.'

When he sent Hall out to bat at No. 3 in their second innings, he was looking for a quick fix. For me, you have an order and you back your batsmen to play. One who can definitely do that is Kallis. He is simply phenomenal, the best batsman in the world. He can play on any wicket against any bowler. He sometimes gets criticised for not scoring fast enough, but we always felt if we could get him out cheaply their order was vulnerable. The two games where he made big runs, his side didn't lose. In the two games we won, he didn't total 100. They aren't a one-man batting line-up, but he gives them a lot of confidence when he gets runs. There is no side in the world he would not get into, he is that good.

After all that had happened, the worries I'd had about my form and the team's unity, I was delighted that I was there when we batted out for the draw which meant we won the series. That gave me an enormous amount of pride. When I sat in the dressing room afterwards, I was just amazed that we had won the series. These had been the hardest weeks of my sporting life. I was surprised that I had been able to bat for three hours at the end because I was knackered. This series meant so much to me because of the amount of abuse we'd taken, because we had overcome not playing well as a collective, because of the criticism we had taken from their media and because there was a lot of ill-feeling between the sides in the last couple of games.

We had come out 2–1 winners so we can't have done that

much wrong. But had we played to our full potential we'd have won 4–1 at least and probably wouldn't have lost a game.

The congratulations came in from people like England's former rugby captain Martin Johnson, the golfers Lee Westwood and Darren Clarke and the Aston Villa manager David O'Leary. It had definitely been a series which had a lot of people glued to the TV back home. I heard that on the last day of the Johannesburg Test the television shops were packed with people clamouring to watch the game. It's great for cricket. I think the England team is the best in the world to watch because you're never quite sure what you're going to get. The number of times we had come back from tricky situations was the key to our success throughout the year. Most of the games could have gone either way, but one after another our players produced when they had to.

13

THE ART OF CAPTAINCY:
What I'd Learnt So Far

The South Africa tour was without doubt the toughest series I had been involved in, but good for my development as a captain. I was still enjoying it although I felt the pressure because I knew we had to go out and not only play well, but win. If we'd have been defeated there we could have written off the Ashes six months ahead of them being played. We would have lost too much confidence.

I always try to think two or three overs in advance and on some occasions I'll try to think a full session ahead. It's a balance because you should also try to play in the present, but you have to judge a wicket and a bowler, how long you can bowl someone, which end, when to introduce spin, that sort of thing.

So I always try to think ahead. We also have different plans for different batsmen. The wicket might not suit the initial plan, so you have to adapt. You have to have plans b and c.

For field placings, I don't go by the book at all. There was a situation at Durban where the stats told me that no catches were going to first slip – the keeper was diving across or the ball wasn't carrying, so we went without a first slip and had second, third and fourth. I don't just put a man there because it's in the rule books. At Johannesburg, we didn't have a second slip and not one ball went there throughout the whole game.

During home games, I will speak to the groundsman beforehand, but all I hope for is the best possible wicket for a Test match. May the best team win. That's what should happen. I don't like doctoring of wickets and I certainly don't want one that deteriorates so much that the toss becomes the crucial part.

I always knew when I got the job that I would have to deal with the media more often, it comes with the territory. I try not to let them wind me up and to be as honest and realistic and calm as I can, but their reaction after our defeat in Cape Town disappointed me. What type of team are they? Was it lucky they won eight in a row? That's the kind of reaction I don't enjoy because we will play badly now and again. We hadn't gone from being a good team to a bad team overnight.

Occasionally I will chat to Nasser or Ian Botham on the morning of a game if they've had a look at the pitch, but we try to do things our own way. If you get opinions from too many people you get confused. Make your decision and go for it is my philosophy.

Our commentators and journalists are, in the main, fair and unbiased. The Sky team has been enhanced by Nasser's move behind the microphone. He seems to have made the transition without any problems and I think he will turn out to be one of the best. He criticises when he feels he has to, but that's through genuine personal opinion rather than any desire to be controversial.

Sky Sports seem to be more aggressive than Channel 4. As for the written press, I have a reasonable working relationship although I don't buy one particular newspaper, picking up all of them from time to time to scan through. Occasionally, you'll find something of interest which is informative, even instructive. Michael Atherton did a piece in the summer of 2004 and he was pretty well spot on about my batting and I was able to learn from it. Other times you have to be strong enough to say, he's criticised me and that's his opinion, but he's not right.

As for the progress of my relationship with Fletcher, it has never been less than good although we both have our opinions about what to do if we win the toss (not usually a problem!), declarations (he's not quite as much of a gambler), tactics and team selection. If we both agreed with one another all the time, you'd get bored and stale. We have the occasional disagreement, but what Duncan always says is you're the captain, we may not agree on this one, but I'll back you, so go with it. On other issues he is in sole command – coaching, preparation and the batting order are all down to him.

It's not just Duncan I talk to though. I always keep in regular contact with the keeper because he gets the best view, while Marcus is good from first slip, as are Flintoff and Thorpe. I like to know that they are all thinking so whatever input they want to make, I'll listen to. I may just go to Keysy at cover and say: 'What do you think?', just to see if his head's screwed on. If he comes up with some load of rubbish then I'll just say: 'Plug in, lad.'

We had great success throughout 2004 – no other Test side remained unbeaten – but that does not mean there are not times when the stresses of the job get to me. Nobody sees what goes on behind closed doors, but there are occasions when I go back to my room, sit down and worry. The important thing is not to let anything get on top of you and if I have a strength in this department it is that when I wake up to a new day it is exactly that, and I can face whatever I have to with a fresh mind.

14

DEFINITELY A PERSONALITY:
Enter Pietersen

We felt that to have won the Test series 2–1 was a fair reflection of how things had gone. Perhaps it should have been 3–1 considering the near-miss in Durban, but we were happy. We played decent cricket, if not our best, while individuals performed at the right time in what had been a very tough and intense series both on and off the pitch. Every day of every Test had swayed one way and then the other and each game went to five days so to come out on top was a reflection of the character of our side. The result said nothing of our youth and that fact filled me with pride and confidence in the future. We were going to get better.

As soon as the Test series finished I was allowed four days off in Johannesburg just to relax my body and mind, and play a bit of golf. My good friend Ashley Giles did the same and we simply chilled out.

The one-day team went off to play a warm-up game which they won quite easily and then the serious one-dayers started in Johannesburg. We won the first, rain-affected match under the Duckworth Lewis system, but we were only chasing 176 before the total had to be altered because of the weather and we were never in trouble.

All the talk, right from the first game, was about the arrival of Kevin Pietersen in our team because he had been born in South Africa, but was qualified to play for England through residency. From the start, he looked a special player with a magnificent eye. I had seen a little bit of him in Zimbabwe, where he proved he could certainly hit the ball, on occasions extremely hard and far.

All the gossip in the media was about how he would react to a baying Wanderers crowd and to the booing when he came out. He answered it superbly. His first few balls were a bit edgy, but for the rest of the series he played better than anybody I had seen in the limited-overs discipline. I don't mean purely recent times, but as long as I have been watching and playing the game. I cannot speak any higher than that. He played four fantastic innings – three 100s and a 75 – and it became evident that we had found a very rare commodity. My thoughts were that I would be very surprised if he did not take this game into the Test-match arena as well.

The second game in Bloemfontein was one of the best and most exciting I have been involved in and truly marked the arrival of Pietersen in the international game. I shared a partnership of 80 with him before he finished on 108 not out, a truly great innings. His hundred came up in just 91 balls and featured two mighty sixes.

We set South Africa 271 for victory and thanks to a partnership of 134 between Jacques Kallis and Herschelle Gibbs, they entered the final over needing just three.

None of us expected the fireworks that followed because Kabir Ali was to bowl the last six balls and his previous seven overs had been expensive. That would be quickly forgotten in an unforgettable finale which saw three wickets fall and the scores finish tied.

Mark Boucher was the first to go when Giles took a catch and then a smart piece of fielding by Ian Bell saw Ashwell Prince run out. South Africa needed one off the last ball with the experienced Andrew Hall facing. In one of the smartest bits of cricket you will ever see, Ali kept his nerve to send down a yorker. Geraint Jones, standing up, took the ball brilliantly to complete a magnificent stumping. We celebrated enthusiastically, to say the least.

It was an amazing game, particularly for me because I had not felt well while batting and collapsed in a state of exhaustion after my innings of 42. I could not field because of what turned out to be a flu virus and Marcus took over for the second half of the match. He did a very good job.

The illness also meant I missed the next game in Port Elizabeth when all our top seven batsmen reached double figures in a total of 267 for eight. It looked like a score we could defend, but Graeme Smith showed that he was quite prolific at one-day level too with an accomplished 105, his first century, and South Africa scraped home with five balls to spare in another exciting game.

We were 1–1 in the series after three matches and looking pretty good, but the long and exhausting schedule finally took a heavy toll and we were trounced in the next match.

Gibbs, a fast scorer and a fierce hitter, scored a hundred while Justin Kemp showed that Pietersen was not alone in being able to hit the ball out of the ground. South Africa reached 291. It was a target we never looked like reaching after losing three wickets for 35 although Pietersen continued to return the criticism of him with interest, smashing 75. It was to no avail. We played badly. Newlands, such a picturesque ground, had not been a good one for us in either discipline.

We were definitely missing the expertise of Flintoff, particularly his bowling, as we moved on to East London. But our top all-rounder's return to England for an ankle operation meant we could give experience to younger players in tough conditions and against a very good one-day side.

Smith again reached a century and Kemp blitzed us with 80 in 50 balls as South Africa reached 311. It was a formidable total, but I dug in for 70 and Pietersen launched one of the fastest one-day international hundreds, but we still ended seven runs short of their total. Pietersen had now scored two centuries and neither time finished on the winning side. We made a decent fist of the chase: some said we didn't attack early enough although after losing two early wickets we had to regroup. In truth, we probably lacked a bit of experience in the bowling department.

We could now only draw the series after going 3–1 down so it was win or bust in Durban and we were beaten, not by South Africa, but the weather. We needed 213 off 48 overs, but only 3.4 were possible. The series was gone, but we had learnt a few things – not least that Alex Wharf was a decent bowler and that Pietersen was something special.

We were tired and several players probably had their mind on the plane home by the time we reached Centurion for the last game. Pietersen was not one of them. Helped by Giles and Kabir Ali hanging around with him, he produced another incredible innings, his 116 including five sixes. Despite this being the end of a long and strenuous tour, we still managed to be competitive. Our 240 looked defendable, but proved otherwise.

However, in Pietersen we found the type of player we had not had in the limited-overs team for a long, long time. I had been won over early because I saw how he enjoyed the whole international arena. He loved the cameras, the bigger crowds, the people watching him practise and play. He also settled into the dressing room nicely, bringing confidence to the side as well as immense ability. I felt that as long as he kept level-headed and worked hard on his game then he would be around for quite a while.

Pietersen scored three hundreds in six innings which is phenomenal in one-day cricket. He hit the ball so cleanly with what looked like a small amount of risk, scoring boundaries at regular intervals, but with shots that were calm and collected rather than dusted with danger. That's the sign of a very good one-day player.

He is definitely a personality and is not lacking in self-confidence. He changes hairstyle as often as David Beckham and enjoys being in the limelight. Anybody who can go out with 40,000 people booing him and perform like he did has got something about him.

15

THE PHONEY WAR:
Waiting for Australia

Zimbabwe and everything that went with it had taken more out of us than we thought and then we went into five almost back-to-back Tests against one of the world's best sides, followed by seven one-day internationals. It's the sort of schedule I hope never to have to go through again. It was too tough on the mind and the body, and very difficult to keep yourself focused and up for every single minute of every game. I was drained by the end of it and, I'll be honest, I was very happy to be able to relax with the family.

Most of the reaction when I got back was positive about the Test series and understanding about the one-dayers. Everybody wanted to know about Pietersen. Would he play against Australia? Would he play with Flintoff? Where would we fit him in? All questions I had to answer a million times, but prompted by the fact that we now had a good team who had reached No. 2 in the world, with the top side coming to visit us very soon.

How are you going to play Australia? Are you going to beat them? Are they over the hill? Are you going to get your form back from the last Ashes? Who? When? Where? Why? What? A two-match series was coming up against Bangladesh, but the non-stop questioning was all about the second part of the summer and the arrival of the Australians. To be honest, by the time the Ashes started I think both teams were pig sick of answering questions and fed up of all the hype and hysteria. We just wanted to get out and play. There's only so much talking you can do about a game of cricket. But everybody was getting ahead of themselves because there was still a lot of cricket to be played before the Ashes.

It was decided because of what we had been through and the summer we had arriving that the guys should get an extended break for rest and recuperation. It would be good to get back to doing normal things because when you are playing you can't get away from it and there are always a myriad of questions to answer. Here was our chance to get away for a while and for me it was an opportunity to chill out with the family, disappear to Barbados for a friend's wedding, play golf and generally do normal things.

We weren't taking extra time out to be unkind to the counties, but only to make sure the England team peaked at the right time. There just isn't the same focus in county cricket. Your mind isn't on scoring runs then, but when the Test matches come around. You don't have the three days' practice before a match starts or the chance to analyse the opposition. It's basically play, play, play from one match to the next.

But the papers have to be full of some kind of rubbish so when the Ashes were approaching and we were all getting 20s and 30s people were writing about how out of form we were. The reality was that we all felt in reasonable touch and were building up nicely to the bigger examinations ahead. The difference is that when you've reached a reasonable score at county level, you feel mentally that you are OK and there's not much to worry about so you might not be totally switched on. At Test level, when you've got yourself in you know you have to go on because you have to make the most of it every single time. There isn't that mental intensity when you're playing for your county and it's not easy for Test players to fit in because you're not there often enough and are governed by a different set of rules, fitting in as best you can.

The Test side is now our 'county' side to a certain extent where we all know our roles within the team, what's expected in training and preparation, and the attitude that we all need to take out on to the pitch. The set-up has been good for the last couple of years and I've stressed that it has to continue.

16

ONE-WAY TRAFFIC:
Bangladesh 2005

The selectors for the Bangladesh series did not have an easy job. Eventually Ian Bell was included, meaning that I moved up from No. 4 to No. 3, a position I have always been comfortable in, where I bat in the one-day game and where I felt I would always end up.

Bell's selection was ahead of Pietersen, or KP as he is known – because of his initials and not because he's a bit of a nut. Graham Thorpe was included and then announced days before the Test that he'd be taking up a position coaching in Australia during the winter and wouldn't be available for the winter tours. It seemed to suggest that he was getting ready to leave international cricket and that hit the selectors by surprise. I'd be lying if I said that initially there wasn't a bit of me which felt that we should get rid of him there and then to give somebody else a chance to gain valuable experience. But then half an hour later I felt that I did want my best team to face Australia and if Graham Thorpe deserved to be in that team then he should be given the opportunity. I knew though that over the next couple of months Thorpe v Pietersen would be a big talking point because it was not a matter of if but when the newcomer would make his entrance. They were nice decisions to have to take, they always are when you have options.

By the time we arrived at Lord's for the First Test against Bangladesh, I was convinced we were ready, not only for them, but for what the rest of the summer had in store. Bangladesh were nothing more or less than I had expected. They were all out in less than 40 overs for 108 on a wicket which looked full of runs. And so it proved. Trescothick, who went on to 194, shared an opening partnership of 148 with Strauss. The middle order (including Thorpe, who unbeknown to any of us including himself, was playing his penultimate Test before retirement) helped themselves to some easy pickings as we rattled up 528 for three declared.

Bangladesh's second innings crumbled to 159, giving us a win by an innings and 261 runs. I'm sure Bangladesh have a future in Test cricket, but at the moment they are not up to that standard and I don't like easy runs at international level. I believe Test matches are called that because they are the ultimate test, and I don't think playing Bangladesh is anything approaching that. I know Sri Lanka weren't world beaters when they started out and yet won the World Cup in 1996. I also know that Bangladesh must gain experience and have to start somewhere, but by being beaten in two days and getting a battering every time they go out, well I'm not sure just how much they are learning from that.

I don't want to harm them or their progress, but I just feel that Test-match hundreds should be hard earned rather than donated. Perhaps there should be a second tier involving the likes of Bangladesh and Zimbabwe (at the moment anyway) plus other countries with aspirations to joining the top nations.

When we arrived at Chester-le-Street for the Second Test I was looking for another two-day win but it's sometimes difficult to get yourselves up mentally for these potential banana skins.

The team produced a good effort in the circumstances – Harmison enjoying his home track with five wickets as Bangladesh were skittled for 104, again in less than 40 overs. Their bowling contained few problems for us and Trescothick helped himself to 151 while Bell and Thorpe shared an unbeaten stand of 187 before I declared.

We missed our two-day target by a few overs. Bangladesh offered far greater resistance than they had previously, three of their players making half-centuries as we won by an innings and 27 runs.

We got as much out of the series as we could, although Flintoff and Geraint Jones not batting was a bit of a negative. But it got to the stage where they weren't going to gain much by batting for an hour against a tired attack.

I still didn't think we'd ever played our 100% game. It may sound weird, but I wasn't even sure we knew just how far we could go. We did realise that we had some very good players and a lot of talent. It was just so important to keep striving, working, enjoying it and not listening too much to whatever is written and said. We knew we were a good side and didn't need other people to tell us. There have been bad days and people have written us off, but we've always had confidence in our ability to come back and more often than not that's what we've done. We knew that we could dig ourselves out of holes, and that if we could get pressure on teams we could win Tests.

I have always stressed the importance of enjoyment, but

that doesn't mean you are not being competitive. When you look at the successful Manchester United football teams all the players look as if they are enjoying themselves and one another's company. When you wake in a morning you should feel that you are fortunate to be getting up to play international cricket so why shouldn't you enjoy it. You practise and prepare as hard as you can, but ultimately you have to enjoy the challenge of playing against good players and teams.

17

ELECTRIC SHOCKS:
The 2005 NatWest Series

We just wanted to get the series against Bangladesh over, and start preparing for the Australians. First was the novelty of a Twenty20 game – a new discipline which I am sure has a huge future. You only have to look at how many it draws through the gate at county level to realise just how much people enjoy it. It attracts a new audience too – couples, kids and people who otherwise might not have been interested. The atmosphere when we beat Australia at the Rose Bowl by 100 runs was the best I have ever experienced in England. I am told that there was a similar electricity generated throughout the country – even at race tracks where they were showing the cricket in between races.

We are not as experienced in limited-overs cricket as many of the top cricketing nations, but we took immediately to this form. Our batsmen entertained the crowd hugely as we reached 179 for eight in our innings. Then Gough and Jon Lewis ripped through the heart of Australia and the tourists fell 100 short. Jason Gillespie was the only player to hit more than 20.

We knew Australia would be a very different proposition in the 50-over games, but they had not had a particularly impressive start to their tour and the hype continued to grow about our chances when the really serious stuff started.

However, the first match of the NatWest Series pitched us against Bangladesh at The Oval and it looked as if they would be steam-rollered again before Aftab Ahmed's growing confidence with the bat left us 191 to chase for victory. It was a task not beyond our openers.

What followed will remain one of the most unbelievable results in cricketing history. Australia were beaten by Bangladesh, a result no one predicted after Ricky Ponting's men reached 249 for five. Bangladesh lost wickets at fairly regular intervals but a stand of 130 between Mohammad Ashraful and Habibul Bashar took them within 50 and they scraped home with four balls to spare. Although I had said throughout the early summer that what happened before the Ashes would have no direct bearing on it, there were plenty of us in the England camp who became Bangladesh supporters for the day. Teams are always looking for whatever kind of edge they can get, particularly against a force such as Australia and no side could have lost such a match without it having some kind of psychological effect. We were hoping for a particularly damaging one, but were realistic enough to understand that the Aussies would bounce back – and sooner rather than later.

Meanwhile, we would be doing everything possible to keep them on the back foot and that is exactly what we did at Bristol. One or two of the Aussies had questioned Steve Harmison, suggesting that they weren't sure what all the fuss was about – although Brett Lee wasn't among them, having felt the full force of a quick, lifting delivery earlier in the tour.

They were soon to realise that they were wrong. Harmison's hostility and control won him five for 33, although Australia still set us a target of 253, mainly thanks to Mike Hussey's 84.

We fell slowly further behind the required rate before Pietersen showed why his Test debut could not be delayed much longer with a majestic 91 not out as we breezed home.

If I had been relatively pleased by my patient 57 in the match, I was less than enamoured by a duck in the next, against Bangladesh at Trent Bridge. But it didn't matter, as we feasted on an inferior attack in our mammoth 391 for four. It was far too many for our opponents.

Injury meant that I was missing when we met Australia again, this time at Chester-le-Street for a day-nighter. It was a game which showed that, after a slow start to the tour, Australia were finally beginning to find some form and particularly Lee and Glenn McGrath, who now looked as if they would be sharing the new ball come Test time.

McGrath is an infuriating bowler because he just nags away at your resolve. I'm sure if you put a dinner plate on a length and just outside off stump he could hit it five times out of six – and closer to the middle than the edge. It's not easy to score and he has the ability to move the ball both ways, in the air and off the pitch. His Test record means that he stands comparison with all the greats. Lee is different. He comes in off a much longer run and is not as accurate as McGrath, but he has matured and can undo batsmen with sheer pace. In the one-day game he is a very effective strike bowler and a key component of Ponting's armoury.

The pair had us in all sorts of early trouble and, chasing 267, we never recovered from being six for three. Flintoff continued to show that he was maturing as a batsman, with some valuable time in the middle, but also as a bowler. The more I saw of him, the more I knew he had fully recovered from his ankle surgery and would be able to trouble the Aussies when the Tests got under way in late July.

Another victory over Bangladesh meant the eighth match of the triangular series was a dead one because both ourselves and Australia had already qualified for the final. Andrew Symonds demonstrated just how brutal a batsman he can be by butchering a run-a-ball 74 – and he can't even get in their Test team – as Australia reached 261. But the weather would be the winner.

And so to Lord's for the final, and what a match, a fitting finale to the first series of the one-day summer. Australia started as if they were in a rush to get to the bar – Adam Gilchrist and Mathew Hayden scoring at seven an over until their first wicket fell at 50. Apart from another half-century partnership, it would be the tourists' only major contribution as we bowled them out for 196.

Our confidence in chasing down the target quickly evaporated as the incomparable McGrath and his one-day sidekick Lee left us on 33 for five in the 10th over.

Cometh the hour cometh two of our smaller, less flashy players. Paul Collingwood has become one of the best one-day cricketers in the world, doing for us what Symonds does for Australia in a different kind of way. He is also arguably the world's best fielder, his flying catch in the Bristol match to dismiss Hayden a contender for take of the century.

Collingwood is also one of the best readers of the game, but he needed an accomplice at Lord's and found one in Geraint Jones, who had taken five catches in Australia's innings. Having gone back down the order after we abandoned the experiment of using him as an opener, he settled in quickly and the pair put on 116 for the sixth wicket.

When Jones followed shortly after Collingwood, we were still 36 short with no recognised batsmen left. What we did have were players willing to give 100% every time. Giles and Darren Gough typified the spirit and took us to just three runs from victory with one ball left.

Giles somehow managed to squeeze the ball out into the off side and, although it was never in danger of reaching the boundary, he and Harmison scrambled the two necessary to force a tie. The body language of the Australians suggested that they thought they had lost the trophy because we had conceded fewer wickets. But the rules stated that in the event of a tie, the trophy would be shared. It was a magnificent match and probably a fair result. Once again we had proved our competitiveness against the best in the world.

18

LIVING WITH THE BEST:
The 2005 NatWest
Challenge

As the hype surrounding the Ashes reached almost insuffer-able proportions, both sides just wanted the big contest to get under way, but there was still unfinished business in the one-day arena. The three-match NatWest Challenge between us and Australia had not even started and we were already into July. It would be another fortnight before the series the cricketing nation was aching for would finally get under way. I suspect that, like us, Australia had just about had enough of one-day cricket, but this was the itinerary we had been set.

So it was to Headingley that we went and the first of the best-of-three series. Without a Test match to look forward to, my home ground was making do with this brief sighting of the Aussies. By their standards, to score at only four runs an over for the first 15 was snail's pace. The opening stand of 62 between Gilchrist and Hayden would be the highest of their innings as Collingwood once again showed how vital he is to our one-day side with four for 34. Our target was 220. It took three of us just 46 overs to seal victory, Trescothick scoring an unbeaten century.

Australia have shown a fondness for Lord's over the years and they cemented their love affair with a very comfortable win to level the series. Only Flintoff, coming nicely into form at a crucial stage of the summer with 87, really caused any problems to the tourists. Few of our bowlers troubled them either and Ponting led his side to victory with a majestic century. He too was looking in ominous form, but I consoled myself with the knowledge that none of these signs could be carried over into the Test matches with any degree of certainty.

The Oval hosted the final game and we disappointed ourselves with just 228 although there were two innings of particular significance. The first and greater was by Pietersen who reminded the selectors of his potential with a patient 74. It was going to be extremely difficult to ignore his claims and I was of the opinion that they should be answered.

Vikram Solanki's 53 not out was different because it came after he had been drafted into the side under new regulations which allowed the use of a substitute. Simon Jones had to make way because we needed more runs than it looked like we were capable of making as the middle order failed.

However, a belligerent 121 from Adam Gilchrist saw Australia home in double quick time. Australia took the series, but we were not down-hearted having shown that we would not be their whipping boys. Also we had won the previous Test between the sides. What we had all been waiting for was now just round the corner. Thank heavens!

19

HELLO, GOODBYE:
The Ashes Begin,
Thorpe Departs

The mighty Aussies, just about unbeatable during my professional life, commanded respect but no fear as preparation for the most eagerly awaited series of the millennium reached its conclusion. Would we be ready for them or was this new, young England team perhaps a year short of its peak? Would the oldest international series finally become a contest instead of a bout of Aussie-inflicted carnage? These were questions which would be answered in the late summer of 2005.

Everybody was asking about Australia, everybody seemed to be talking about the Ashes. Even a year before the first ball was bowled, it was apparent that Ashes Fever was turning into an epidemic in the British and Australian cricketing worlds. Little did I appreciate that once the battle started many people who did not know a maiden over from a maiden century would also become engrossed.

Every time we won a game, even one months in advance, people would say: 'Is that how you'll play against Australia?' Every time we had a bad day, they'd say: 'There's absolutely no chance against Australia if you play like that.' If we did well, then they'd say: 'We might do OK against Australia, but we have to improve.'

Everything, no matter who we were playing, was geared towards how we would tackle the Aussies. Game plans, team personnel: people wanted to know exactly how we intended to win back the Ashes after the best part of 20 years. The obsession with the battle ahead probably started after we'd won in the West Indies during the winter of 2003–04. People were beginning to believe that we might have a team capable of achieving something special.

Wins against New Zealand and West Indies at home fuelled the speculation, but people seemed to think that the real yardstick was how we fared against South Africa in the southern hemisphere. If we beat them then perhaps we had a chance against the world champions. If not, forget it.

I too understood the importance of doing well against South Africa. It was a huge series for us because I knew we were at a similar stage of development to them. I knew it would be a huge achievement if we could go down there and win.

The fact that we once again realised our dreams and broke records not only enhanced the team's standing, but also intensified the interest in the arrival of Ricky Ponting and his baggy-green brigade. I wasn't 100% sure we were ready for them, wondering if perhaps they were coming a year too soon. But I did know that the team was full of talent, fight and enthusiasm. We were not going to roll over, and we were going to get better even before the Aussies arrived. We had to because a nation expected.

To win 2–1 in South Africa gave me a belief that we could

play well against Australia. I also realised that we would still have to go up another gear. I still felt that we would have to play beyond ourselves, if that was possible, to win the Ashes.

Players would have to grab hold of the game at crucial times and produce brilliant performances. Collectively we would have to play like we had never done before. I dedicated myself to ensuring that everything that could be done would be. The line-up of the team was coming together as the curtain-raising visit by Bangladesh approached.

Thorpe announced that he would not be available for the winter tours because he had accepted a coaching job in Australia. His announcement came as a surprise because I had a feeling he would make clear his intentions at the end of the summer and not the beginning. He was looking after his long-term future. He wrote in his book that he thought I was a little naïve in asking him at Lord's before we played Bangladesh, his 99th Test, whether or not he'd get through the summer because of his suspect back.

I only asked him because I wanted the team that faced Bangladesh to be the one that was picked against the Aussies. Bell had arrived in international cricket as if he had been born to it while Pietersen, who looked like missing out if Thorpe was fit, was knocking on the door hard. If Thorpe wasn't going to be facing Australia, then I couldn't see any reason for him playing against Bangladesh, no matter how close to 100 caps he was.

Reaching that milestone is a great achievement, but I wasn't going to sacrifice the team's interests. When you're about to face Australia the whole emphasis has to be on what is best for the team. Ideally I did not want Kevin making his Test debut against Australia so if there was doubt about

Thorpe's back then it was better for the team if he made way early. It did not turn out that way.

Thorpe did go on to receive his 100th cap, against Bangladesh, but there would be no more. A few weeks later Pietersen was selected ahead of him for the first Ashes Test and one day into the game Thorpe announced his retirement from international cricket.

I believe it was the right move to select Pietersen because it meant we were going into the series with young players who had no fear. They didn't have experience, OK, but experienced cricketers had played against the Aussies for 16 years and we hadn't really achieved much. A young team could do no worse.

20

FALSE START:
Lord's 2005

We played well in the one-dayers, but for me the crucial turning point of the summer was the first Twenty20 game between the sides, at Hampshire's Rose Bowl ground. After the game I publicly talked down its importance, but beforehand in the dressing room I talked it up, as did Duncan. We spoke about the importance, right from ball one, of not letting Australia intimidate us. We had to be in their faces and show them that we were a different side mentally to any they had played.

It may have been a gimmick of a game, but I firmly believe that the Twenty20 victory – when we pulverised them – induced a few shivers in their dressing room and sent a message that we weren't going to be intimidated and would be aggressive with them. Still, however easy it had been over an hour and a half in a 20-over match, the big test was whether we could now do it over 50 overs and, more important, over four or five days. I will admit that at that stage I still had doubts.

We kept on asking the side what they thought they could achieve, but no matter how positive the response, I knew that we were inexperienced. To keep asking them to be disciplined, to sustain the intensity of their approach and preparation, to take the pressure of an Ashes series at home, was going to be a big ask. I felt we could do it for a couple of games, but for five in a row against the best was going to be something colossal. It would be character defining.

There were really good signs during the one-day series. We'd got over the line at Bristol, beaten them at Headingley and tied the final after being in a bad position. Players seemed to be enjoying the challenge of Australia whereas in the past – certainly when I'd played down there – there were players who had been daunted. The feeling of 'Hell, we're playing Australia. What are we going to do?' had now disappeared. To a man, we were stimulated by the prospect of playing the world champions. The mentality was: 'Right, we'll give you a game. You don't intimidate us because you're only human. We respect you, but you don't frighten us.'

We intended to prove to them that they were not invincible, that they could be beaten. I felt that it would be vital to sustain the pressure over long periods. If you have a bad day against them then the game can disappear very quickly so we could not afford to have many bad sessions.

I liked the composition of the team. I'd seen enough of Bell to realise he was a composed player, and he had done well against Bangladesh. I really think he's the way forward and part of the future of English cricket. What an opportunity it was for him to play in an Ashes series when he was so young, particularly at home with all the pressure of media and everybody's expectations. It's a lot easier abroad.

The hype had built to unprecedented levels and I could sense that both camps just wanted to get on with it. By July little comments were being blown out of all proportion to their significance. Glenn McGrath, not for the first time, had his say and predicted an Aussie whitewash and Hoggard replied. Little did he realise that his aside about one or two Aussies entering the autumn of their careers would become headline news.

McGrath's comments drove me on more than anything else because I did not want this England team to be embarrassed in their own backyard. I knew how much progress we had made over two years and I knew how much damage a heavy series defeat could inflict. I also knew we had it within ourselves to play well, put them under pressure and maybe nick an early game.

The build up to the First Test at Lord's was as nerve-racking as I had ever experienced because of the hype and the pressure of where we were playing and the opposition facing us. I slept all right, but I could feel the tension within the squad. They were not over-awed, but they were feeling the situation. I told them not to look too far ahead and just concentrate on day one. That would set up the rest of the game. If we could get that out of the way and start on top, the game could look after itself. I knew the first session in recent Ashes series had left England behind: we had to concentrate on the first one. We knew our plans and they included getting in the Aussies' faces and not being intimidated. That was all anybody could ask. What I got was more than I had expected or hoped for.

On day one, with a packed and expectant Lord's not believing what it was seeing, Australia went in for lunch at 97 for five. Even I had to pinch myself, but, yes, the best team in the world had had their top order knocked over for next to nothing.

Hoggard started the slide when a perfect in-swinger knocked back Hayden's off stump. Ricky Ponting, a key man, followed shortly afterwards when he could do no more than fence Harmison's wicked lifter to Strauss at third slip.

Justin Langer went to pull Flintoff and skyed a catch to square leg, while Damien Martyn was beaten by Jones's out-swing and was taken behind. The Aussies were 66 for four and every man in our four-strong pace attack had taken a wicket. Simon Jones became the first to take two when he trapped Michael Clarke lbw and we were a very happy bunch when lunch arrived.

We were even happier before tea because Australia were in the field having been dismissed for 190 as Harmison helped himself to five. The thing about Australia is that they always come back hard, but even we didn't expect just how difficult McGrath would be to cope with. He was almost unplayable. He reduced us to 21 for five, celebrating his 500th Test victim when Trescothick felt first ball after tea.

We were staring at humiliation until Pietersen, on his Test debut, and Geraint Jones steered us toward respectability. Pietersen proved just how big a talent and personality he has by hitting a half-century and the tail wagged to such an extent that we finished just 35 behind.

Now we needed to bowl and field as well as we could. We didn't and Australia clawed their way to 384, giving them a lead that was always going to be big enough. Had we held our chances and restricted them to an advantage of about 250, I'm sure we could have chased it down. It was not to be and the critics emptied themselves of hope and filled their pens with poison.

We'd started so well, better than myself or anybody else

had expected. That really settled us down, but unfortunately the wicket suited McGrath perfectly and he came out with one of the best spells of his career. At the end of a first day when 17 wickets had fallen, everybody knew that this Ashes series was going to be very special indeed.

So there were huge positives. The only negative had been on the Saturday morning in the field when for the only time I felt we were slightly intimidated by the Aussies. As I looked round and saw the concerned look of the players, I knew this was something we had to address very quickly because a feeling of 'Oh Hell! Here we go again' could not be tolerated at such an early stage of the series. I couldn't understand it because most of the team hadn't been there before so they shouldn't have been feeling like that. It was as if they were starting to believe what was being written in the press.

I remember Steve Howard in *The Sun* after day one having a real go at us: another England team, another disaster, no chance. I thought this was very unfair when you consider how far we had come. I knew that this England team was good enough to make him eat his words.

I tried after the game to be as honest and level as I could. I told the side that the only problem was that we believed too much of the hype and hadn't handled the pressure situations well enough. Our minds were elsewhere and we were thinking about what was being written and what the crowd was saying. When we started thinking too much our performance level dropped. We produce our best cricket when we just go out and play on instinct, with discipline and enjoyment.

I told them we had 10 days to regroup: don't pay any attention to the rubbish that will be written, be strong, make sure we come back as a fresh team, one that is ready to have another go. People were saying when we went 1–0 down that we'd lost the Ashes already, but that wasn't the case.

Before the First Test we'd had the explorer Dave Mill give us an hour's presentation on how he got through an unsupported walk to the North Pole – an amazing journey of endurance, skill and strength. There were parallels to be shared and he told us there would be blips and setbacks along our route. After the First Test I remembered what he'd said.

When I looked at the game in general terms I didn't feel we'd played badly. I saw a couple of sessions where McGrath bowled an unbelievable spell and was virtually unplayable. We dropped some crucial chances and allowed them to get too big a lead, but there were occasions when we put them under a lot of pressure.

I just emphasised the positives. The start we made was positive; Pietersen's debut had been very impressive and Harmison's bowling outstanding so there was nothing to be too downhearted about. I looked around the dressing room after it was over and the team was down, as you'd expect having lost heavily to Australia, but I knew it was something of a release to have got the first game out of the way. The pressure might have been relieved because no longer would we be expected to win. We'd come back before and I was confident we would do it again. Edgbaston would be our biggest test.

Personally, I'd had two low scores when I'd got out to balls I hadn't been able to do much about – two skidding low bounces. If you're playing well or not, you're still going to get out to them. Mentally I remained strong despite my poor start. I wasn't going to read the rubbish in the press;

instead I focused on the positives because I had actually felt pretty good in the middle.

I knew I had the chance to go away and work on my batting. I decided against playing for Yorkshire in a four-day game and instead worked one-to-one with Duncan Fletcher in the nets. The experts in the newspapers suggested that wasn't the right way to go about it, but I knew what I needed to do. I had to have a few days off, a few days practice and then a one-day game where I went and got a century for Yorkshire. That was pleasing knowing that I had put the work in and then got somewhere.

Quite a few people asked me why Ponting had such a verbal go at me when I went out to bat, believing it was because neither I nor any of the team went over to enquire about his health when he'd been felled by a Harmison bouncer earlier. Harmison's bowling throughout that First Test, following criticism of his performances in South Africa, was magnificent. He made quite a few Aussies play through the pain barrier, the mood set in the very first over when Langer took a nasty blow off a totally legitimate ball. Hard, relentless, but fair was what we were about. I felt that their batsmen knew they were going to be in for a hard time from our bowling attack and it was our aim not to disappoint them. They knew they were going to have to fight for every run, that there would be very few cheap ones.

Our tactic is to play aggressively, and by hitting somebody you can affect the way they play, but nobody likes to see someone injured on the field. Ponting got up quite quickly after Harmison hit him on the helmet and although there was a bit of claret trickling down his face, it wasn't too serious. Had we felt it was serious, we'd all have gone over.

It wasn't our reaction that had got under Ponting's skin, but my throwing in to the keeper. He felt I'd thrown at Shane Warne, a belief I wasn't going to give any credibility to by replying. He let me know that I could expect plenty of the same and that I could expect to be hit, but I just laughed it off.

I think they'd been wound-up during the one-dayers, when Simon Jones had thrown at the stumps and hit Hayden. In fact they'd had bees in their bonnet all summer about little issues. And they call us whingeing Poms? The throwing in and our use of substitutions really seemed to have got to them, but I found it difficult to understand what they were complaining about. If a man's out of his ground we are perfectly entitled to throw at the stumps and as for substitutions, Australia haven't been slow to use them. They were riled, however, and when you get the Aussies riled you know you have done something right.

Ever since I took over the captaincy I have always stressed how lively I wanted us to look in the field. I wanted us to be intense and never blasé. I told them that every time you get the ball wing it in to the keeper as quickly and as hard as you can. I also told people to run in between overs to show the opposition how positive we are, how much energy we've got. There was no reason why we shouldn't because we're still so young and fit. It's the same with our batting when we look to be positive all the time.

I've always felt there has been a fear of failure against Australia, certainly in my playing time. It's almost as if players have been scared to put themselves on the line. They can be that good that they can embarrass you but I did not want any of that fragile mentality now and our attitude to fielding was part of the new approach.

I also wanted a consistency of selection. I felt if we could keep the same group of players together we would have a much bigger chance than if we were constantly swapping because the whole approach changes when that happens. There were calls after the First Test for Bell and Geraint Jones to be dropped, while Giles also came in for some flak. Thankfully the selectors resisted all temptation. I was happy with the team we had and I was determined that we would win or lose with that unit.

Some of the criticism of Giles was of a particularly unnecessary nature and repugnant odour and he felt inclined to answer back when, in retrospect, I think he realised he would have been better taking it on the chin.

When I arrived at Edgbaston on the Tuesday, Giles looked a haggard man. He looked like he'd been through the mill for a few days so I sat him down and told him to do nothing more now than concentrate on what he did on the field. There had to be no outside distractions. I felt he'd wasted a lot of energy worrying about things and getting embroiled in an argument which ran and ran. I asked him to have no other focus than his cricket and to realise that when you lose there will always be criticism and praise when you win. As a nation of critics we see something as great or crap, with not much in between. Giles now realises that you really do have to keep your mouth shut and let your cricket do the talking . . . and that's exactly what he did.

His reaction on the field was always going to be a test of his character and I had no doubt he would come through it. He'd never experienced a week of media attention like it before, but now he had to get back out into the middle.

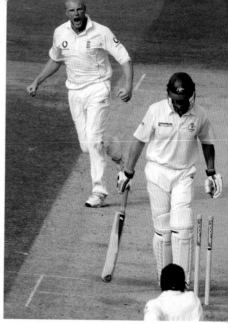

'Yes,' they said, 'but can we beat the Aussies?' I've always been very confident myself – being interviewed before the first Ashes Test, July 2005.

It all started so well – Adam Gilchrist falls to Freddie Flintoff for 26. Australia were all out for 190 in their first innings.

The coiled spring of cricketing history – Lord's, day one. Steve Harmison bowls the first ball of the 2005 Ashes series.

Few have come back from injury as Simon Jones has done. Here he cleans up the Australian tail at Lord's.

Starting as he meant to finish, Kevin Pietersen lofts McGrath into the Lord's pavilion on day two – and we still lost.

Waiting for the third umpire's decision in the Second Test at Edgbaston – I had run out Damien Martyn all right.

Ashley Giles had received a lot of stick after our Lord's debacle. This was the man's reply – five priceless wickets at Edgbaston.

Kevin Pietersen and I mob wicket-taker Ashley Giles. The players really do buy into the team ethic.

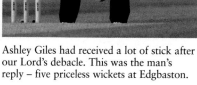

The nation narrowly avoids a collective heart-attack. Australia needed just 3 runs for victory at Edgbaston when Steve Harmison had Michael Kasprowicz caught behind.

Top row: On the way to 166 at Old Trafford and the end of a worryingly bad trot for me. England's commanding first-innings score of 444 left Australia facing something they don't like, and don't often have to play – a chase game.

Below left: Strauss reverse sweeps his way to his first Test century against Australia.

Below: Shane Warne, caught Jones, bowled Flintoff – who is about to detonate.

Cranking up for Trent Bridge. People said the psychological edge would be against us – I didn't understand their reasoning.

I will admit that this summer was the hardest I have ever known in my professional life.

Marcus Trescothick drives Michael Kasprowicz to build us a sound start at Trent Bridge.

Flintoff was simply a massive player for us. This was his first Test century against Australia, and very classy and controlled it was too. We were in the Fourth Test driving seat with 477.

Not since 1988 had the Aussies been asked to follow on. Hoggard dismisses Michael Clarke for 56. Give him the conditions and there is no finer swing bowler.

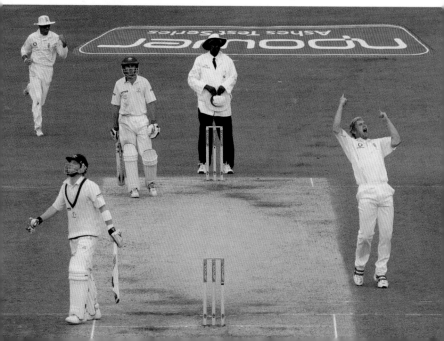

Above: More jubilation as Gilchrist goes and Andrew Strauss is hoisted in the air by big Fred. All we needed now was 129 runs for victory –which, as you know, would not be a problem…

Right: He can win them on his own. The wizard Warne very nearly did for us in our second innings at Trent Bridge.

Below: Definitely not amused – being run out by substitute Gary Pratt in his second innings leaves Ricky Ponting far from speechless.

21

THE GREATEST TEST:
Edgbaston 2005

The atmosphere among the team when we arrived at Edgbaston on the Tuesday before the match was very good and Fletcher sat everybody down in the team room and spoke about Lord's and all the positives we could take out of the defeat. All I added was to point out that we had enjoyed our cricket over the last two years and now that we were all under pressure there was no reason why we should not go out and take pleasure in the atmosphere of playing in the second city. It had always been a good ground for us, and the crowd fantastic, so I just wanted us to give it a good go by enjoying our preparation while looking forward to Thursday. There had to be no 'Here we go again' attitude, just a positive outlook.

I thought the vibe in the camp in the build-up to the match was excellent, but I was a little worried that Giles would come in for more stick as the game got nearer especially since he would be now operating on his own ground. Fate stepped in, in the shape of a Chris Tremlett lifter which struck me such a blow while practising that I was convinced my arm was broken. I couldn't feel my left arm at all, and when I could the pain was intolerable so I was carted off for a scan.

Fortunately there was no break, just swelling, and I knew within hours that I would be OK to play. When I woke up the following morning the papers were full of what had happened and in a funny kind of way I was pleased I had been hit by that ball. The attention had moved from Giles to whether the captain would be fit. My elbow would become the focus rather than whether Giles could bowl, bat or field.

I was fit, and when fate stepped in again it had swapped camps. Once we were out on the field warming up the focus was now on McGrath, who was being carried off with a twisted ankle after stepping on a ball. I didn't think too much about it because I knew that whatever XI Australia put out, it was going to be a tough and disciplined unit. McGrath or no McGrath, we knew it was still going to be very hard for us and that we must improve our performance.

Ours was the same XI as at Lord's. Eight or nine of us had played badly there but I would have been upset if anybody had been singled out and dropped. I saw no reason to bring out the chopping board although there were calls from some quarters to bring back Thorpe. That was never an option for me. He'd decided to retire from international cricket and once you've done that, you stick with it. As I saw it, we'd failed together at Lord's. It was not an individual error so we deserved the chance to put that right at Edgbaston.

That opportunity was offered us and we prepared for another sell-out match determined to show the Aussies exactly what we were made of. How good it was is for the thousands there and millions more watching on television to determine, but it was eventually dubbed The Greatest Test. Whether it was or not, who knows, but it was certainly a great test of nerve, resolve, patience, stamina and just about everything else you can think of.

Ponting once again won the toss, but he must have seen something we didn't because this time he elected to bowl. We would have batted so the toss became an irrelevance. We wanted first use of a slow wicket because we knew from past experience that Edgbaston can spin quite a lot on days four and five and sometimes even day three so Warne would be a big factor. But now we wouldn't be batting last against him and that was something of a relief, although we appreciated that it doesn't matter when you face him – he would always present the ultimate challenge.

It was important that we put them under pressure by getting runs on the board. They came thick and fast from Trescothick and Strauss who put us on course for our target of 400, and the game could not have been that old when Ponting first started wondering if he had made the right decision at the toss. The manner in which we played on that first day was for me the turning point of the entire series.

For us to go out and smash 407 in 80 overs was exactly the right tonic after the defeat at Lord's and gave everybody a lift. It showed we could compete against them.

We had 112 on the board before our first wicket fell – Strauss bowled by one from Warne which turned the best part of a yard and invoked memories of his first delivery against England, the Mike Gatting miracle ball. Then Kasprowicz got Trescothick to nick one behind when he'd made 90 and when Bell followed in similar fashion and I'd gone to a boundary catch, we were suddenly 187 for four and not in as good a shape as we had hoped. There would be another 103 on the board before our fifth wicket went down as

Pietersen and Flintoff shared their first century partnership. Do not bet against them adding many more. All the tail went into double figures to take us past 400 and we had cause to be optimistic. A lot of people thought it was only a par score, but I knew the runs were on the board and their batsmen were under pressure to get past our total. With our attack, it would not be easy for them – and so it proved.

Cricket in the modern era involves a lot of statistical analysis and we had done our homework on every one of their players. The knowledge allows me to set certain fields for individual players, but even I was surprised when Hayden fell into the trap of failing to resist driving the first ball he received. To the delight of the bowler Hoggard and everybody else, it went straight into the safe hands of Strauss at short extra cover.

Australia had reached 88 before the second wicket fell – Giles was the gleeful recipient of a much-needed wicket when Ponting top-edged to me round the corner. The speed at which every England player surrounded Giles showed him exactly what we'd thought of the criticism of him. This team is a very close-knit group and when one feels pain we all do. We were all delighted for Giles, particularly since it was such a prize scalp which came at a time when it looked like they were really getting into the game.

I managed to sneak a run-out just before lunch so we left the field in very good spirits indeed. Australia, thanks mainly to Clarke and Gilchrist, were just able to get past 300, giving us a handy lead of 99. We knew this was a very good position and intended to make the most of it. On that kind of surface, it was a great effort.

The wicket was starting to show signs of wear and we

knew that Warne would be a handful in our second innings. He had a superb ally in Lee, not the last time this pair would share a splendid partnership in the match, although the next time they would be in tandem would be with bats in hand and victory in mind.

Our second innings was memorable for two things both involving the incomparable Freddie Flintoff. His 73 was a magnificent effort and his last-wicket stand of 51 with Simon Jones was crucial. Lee and Warne had us at 131 for 9 before our last pair added the runs that would prove decisive. We had a lead of 281 – not as many as we would have liked but enough, we felt, to defend.

What happened next was extraordinary, prompting the 'Greatest Test' claims. We knew the last two sessions on Saturday could be series defining. If they won to go 2–0 with three to play then our chances would have been slimmer than a catwalk model. We had to win, but little did we appreciate just how tough it would be and just how many hearts Australia would set pounding on the Sunday morning.

When they reached 47 without loss I was starting to think: 'Oh, my word' or something to that effect. Step forward Flintoff. Freddie splattered Langer's stumps and then Ponting edged behind in the same over and suddenly we were ascendant again. Wickets tumbled regularly and when nightwatchman Gillespie became Freddie's third victim, Australia were 137 for seven with almost another 150 needed.

It was another 38 runs before the next wicket fell, but it was as valuable as it gets – Harmison removing Clarke with the best slow ball I had ever seen. It was also the last delivery of the day and brought victory into ever clearer vision. We'd claimed the extra eight overs in a bid to force victory that evening, but surely the inevitable had only been delayed overnight. Australia needed another 107 to win with Warne and Lee at the crease and just Kasprowicz to come. Surely it was a task beyond them. Surely we would level the series. Surely the unthinkable could not happen. Surely became might, became oh, became what on earth is going on during two hours of drama the likes of which had not been seen at Edgbaston for many a year, if ever.

The match could have been over in just two balls on the Sunday morning, but not one seat was empty when we came out to finish them off. This was just how much an English crowd wanted to see the Aussies beaten. The whole country was in the grip of cricket fever that week and it seemed that everybody had suddenly realised that we had a team capable of beating Australia after all these years. The crowd at Edgbaston is always great, but they were simply fantastic that week. The strength and depth of support was something I had never experienced before.

Warne and Lee rode their luck while their bodies took a battering in the process. Nobody was terribly perturbed when the required number clicked down and when Warne was forced so far on to the back foot by a hostile Flintoff that he trod on his stumps, Australia were still 62 short of victory.

Not long after, every coronary unit within 100 miles was put on red alert as Lee and Kasprowicz staged one of the fightbacks of all time. Lee is a wonderful cricketer and sportsman. He runs in time after time when he's bowling, has a big heart when he bats and hits a clean ball. He's no mug and even though there weren't many parts of his body that hadn't been hit, he refused to succumb while Kasprowicz was a magnificent foil.

There was more than one occasion when I said to myself: 'This can't be happening.' But I stuck with my belief in Flintoff and Harmison. If anybody could finish off Australia, one of them could.

The knot of yellow-shirted Australian fans seemed to grow in number and voice as the run countdown continued. But, funny as it might seem, the closer they got to our total, the more I felt chances to get one of them out would come, because they too would start feeling the pressure. When Simon Jones spilled a very difficult chance at third man, I wondered if that was the opportunity gone, and whether fate was to deliver the cruellest of blows. The vastly outnumbered visiting fans were almost deafening as they too contemplated the unthinkable.

The tail-end heroes needed just two to tie when Harmison came pounding in from the Pavilion End for the last time. Kasprowicz fended at a lifter and gloved the ball behind. Geraint Jones was alive to where it had gone and threw himself forward, just managing to get his glove beneath the ball before it reached the ground.

Jones ran to answer the previous taunts of the Australian fans, we engulfed him and Harmy, Lee sank to his knees at coming so close yet so far and Freddie quite rightly took man-of-the-match honours. We might have scraped home by the skin of Kasprowicz's gloves, but we were now 1–1 and all talk of a 5–0 whitewash had been dismissed as claptrap.

I knew there would be questions about my captaincy concerning why I'd kept my players out on the boundary, but I wanted to take the game on as long as I could. I had to try to stop the boundaries because I knew they would hurt us more than anything at that stage. Lee hit one to deep cover when they needed four and if I'd had everybody in saving one and his shot had gone a yard either side of cover then they would have won the game. Two balls later we trapped Kasprowicz so it was a gamble I felt justified in taking. I don't think there is a right or wrong thing to do in those situations. You just need a bit of luck to go your way and it did. Harmy bowled a great ball, Geraint took a great catch, we levelled the series and Edgbaston went bananas. Meanwhile the rest of Britain was talking cricket again.

22

SO NEAR, AND YET...:
Old Trafford 2005

Throughout the three and a half days at Edgbaston we felt we had done enough to deserve the victory no matter how close the eventual outcome had been. Despite what might have been written, particularly in Australia, we did not leave the Midlands in any way scarred by the trauma of the last morning, when the tourists' last pair took so long to dislodge.

People can talk about psychological advantage, as they had all summer, but when you have two good and well-matched teams, every new game starts from square one and not from the situation of the previous match. The idea of momentum doesn't really apply because each team has it within themselves to play better than the other on any given day. For us, it was just comforting to be back in the series.

It had been a collective effort, but nobody had captured the nation's attention more than the man of the match, Freddie Flintoff. He'd been a hero to me for the previous two years, but it looked like the country had finally found him and were willing to launch him to superstar stature – a true sporting hero.

Freddie was a lot more relaxed during the summer and

maybe that's because he just went out and enjoyed playing cricket the way he does. He was also very focused on the pitch, no more so than when bowling – an aspect of his game which was very impressive as I'm sure the Aussies would testify. He just kept running in and putting the ball in the right areas and followed plans to the exact detail, particularly when operating against left-handers. Flintoff is simply a massive player for us, one who knows how important his role is and just wants to bowl more and more. He's for ever saying, 'Let me have a bowl' and as soon as we take a wicket he'll say: 'Right, do you want me on now?' It's always a good to have such a willing and committed player.

Freddie could bowl with the new ball, but he could also be wasted with it. He bowls that well when the ball's 10 overs old that it might not be in the team's best interests to let him have it from the off. Harmison and Hoggard bowl well with the new ball, Simon is becoming good with it, and it's nice to know that Freddie's still to come and will be just as dangerous if not more so. If we have him in hand and get a couple with the new ball then what a bowler to come on and create havoc! Even if we don't force an early break-through, Freddie will create opportunities whenever he bowls. I think the position we use him in now is just about perfect. This was his first series against Australia and he certainly enjoyed the experience. As Kevin Keegan might say: 'He loved it.'

After Edgbaston, many of the lads just went home to rest for Monday and Tuesday, but it was difficult to escape cricket. The nation seemed to be thinking and talking about nothing else. Viewing figures were going through the roof and we had become a cricketing nation again – front page, back page and in between. I just hoped that all the squad would be able to get away from it to clear their heads and heal their bodies in time for a new start at Old Trafford on the Thursday. It had been a very intense game at Edgbaston and if all they were thinking about was cricket then their minds could easily get frazzled during the second of this back-to-back pair of matches. I came home, chilled out and did very little before we got back together on the Wednesday for some light practice.

Duncan Fletcher spoke for a while at our team meeting in the evening; Ashley put his music on to accompany some of the video footage from Edgbaston and I told them that we had now done it once and there was no reason why we shouldn't do it again. We had to ensure we performed to that level consistently. It was not going to be just a one-off. I was sure that they believed they could produce that form week-in, week-out. We had been doing it for two years and just because it was now Australia we were facing didn't mean we couldn't continue in the same vein. There was a positive vibe about the team room.

The talk elsewhere was whether Lee would be fit and indeed McGrath, whom we had not missed at all at Edgbaston. We took no notice because I insisted throughout the summer that all we would do was concentrate on our own performance. It was no use wondering about something we had no influence over. How we reacted, prepared and played: these were things we could do something about.

I felt a great confidence running through the team. It was wonderful to see Trescothick showing self-belief because it had not always been the case for him with Australia. He had not got a hundred against them yet, but it didn't look far away. In previous Ashes series he had looked almost intimidated and definitely somewhat overawed. That was no longer there. All summer he had looked so controlled and assured and when you see him like that you know he's going to get runs. It was no surprise to me that he has been our most consistent player for a long while now, a real jewel for any captain. He really did seem to have the mental side sorted against the best team and that was a great sign.

Leading into the match, Tres was playing well and although Strauss and myself hadn't got many, I knew there were runs around the corner. Whether you are in a bad trough or on a good run, they all have to end somewhere and I felt ours were about to. I had a firm belief I wasn't far off finding something as long as I continued digging deep. I'd worked hard on the psychology part of the game and watched old videos of the times when runs came frequently. I just kept telling myself that I was a good player and that there wasn't much wrong, although the entire nation seemed to be talking about my technique for a week. I didn't really listen to anything or read about it because I knew there wasn't much to talk about. It was just a lot of people making mountains out of molehills. There wasn't much wrong as long as I continued to believe.

On the morning of the match Australia included Lee and McGrath, as we expected, but I knew we were ready to face anything they threw at us. My attitude had been changed by meeting a six-year-old Manchester boy called Connor who was a survivor of several heart operations and was the mascot as I went out for the toss. I remember looking at him and wondering: 'What have I got to worry about?' There I am thinking that I haven't got many runs for four innings and here's a young kid only surviving because of a series of major operations including a transplant. It certainly relaxed me, and encouraged me just to go out and play as I knew I could – on instinct and see where it took me. We won the toss and batted well and once again we were in a position to dominate.

Trescothick had already given notice of his intent before Strauss became Lee's first victim with the score on 26 and that brought me together with my old opening partner. What a joy it was to share a century partnership with him.

I'd spoken the night before the match about the fact that nobody had scored a hundred on either side so it was particularly pleasing that I was able to be the first and that Strauss would be the second when we batted again. We could have done without the third coming from Ponting on the last day.

I lost Tres when he'd scored 63 and we were 163, but Bell showed his potential and class and when I got out after four hours 40 minutes there were already 290 on the board and seven wickets to fall. The manner in which I played showed the rhythm and style I had grown accustomed to over the last few years and it was particularly gratifying to know that I had put the team in a strong position. It was the perfect start. I had been dropped behind and bowled off a McGrath no-ball in successive deliveries, but you need your luck. In four previous innings I'd received three decent balls out of four so I felt my luck had to change somewhere.

Flintoff and Geraint Jones weighed in with valuable contributions and when our last wicket fell, not one going to McGrath, we had 444 to play with. Some people felt we should have got more, but that total is a good one on any wicket, a lot of runs, a lot of time out of the game and they were immediately under pressure – again.

On the following day, we bowled as well as we had for a

long time. We were a unit and Simon Jones sent down a very impressive spell and was rewarded with six wickets. Warne hurt us, but he was the only one. Seven of their players got starts, but only Warne went on, falling just 10 short of a maiden Test century.

Warne's innings proved that it was still a fantastic wicket so for us to get a lead of 142 was a tremendous effort. It allowed us to go out and bat in a very positive manner. Strauss got a great hundred and Belly, under pressure going into the match, completed his second half-century of the game allowing me to declare on 280 for six, a lead of 422.

We felt just over a day was enough time to bowl them out because they had only survived 84 overs in the first innings and we now had 108 at our disposal. I didn't mind dangling half a carrot because they knew if they batted out of their skins then they had a chance of winning. If they had that thought in their heads then I knew it would create a few more chances for us.

The Manchester rain had already played its part and we lost almost a day which would ultimately prove crucial. After getting Langer early, Ponting came in and we would not see the back of him until the ninth wicket fell. We bowled nicely, but a couple of chances went down, they made the most of their luck and we had four overs at their last pair. Unfortunately Lee and McGrath would not be moved.

We were disappointed not to have taken the lead in the series, but I pulled the team together at the end and congratulated them on another great Test. I told them to look at how enthusiastically Australia were celebrating a draw, a rare sight in cricket and an indication that we were now the more dominant force in the series.

The crowd had been as good as they had been at Edgbaston and thousands were locked out on the last day. It was just another fantastic Test to have been part of, but the nine-day break between matches was very welcome. Both teams were both mentally and physically drained from their efforts after so many intense days.

There is a lot of respect and friendship between the two sets of players although it is played very hard in the middle. They are such a tough side to beat and we're a team who just keep having a go and producing good performances.

People said that to draw after coming so close to victory meant the psychological effect would be against us, but I didn't understand their reasoning. For three days at Edgbaston we had been in control and for four days at Old Trafford we had completely dominated so why should there be a down side to that. The positive approach we had shown and the manner in which we had dominated were surely plus factors in our favour. It could only stand us in good stead for the next match. The next challenge was whether we could do it again at Trent Bridge. I was confident that we could.

23

ADVANTAGE ENGLAND:
Trent Bridge 2005

Shane Warne is the greatest spinner cricket has ever known so he was always going to be a handful. For me, it was the manner in which we played him which was going to be more important than how he bowled against us. We weren't going to be intimidated or fearful about him beating the bat now and again with a good leg-break. I wanted us to look to score off him rather than concentrate on defence. That was our approach throughout the summer, not just with Warne, but also McGrath. We knew they would bowl the unplayable now and again, but they wouldn't be right on the money every ball and when our chance came we had to take it. We had to find ways of scoring against them while finding a way to defend the good balls.

There were other areas where we wanted to make runs and one of those was by running hard between the wickets. They didn't seem to be quite as athletic as they were two years previously and I wanted us to pressure them in the field. With Gillespie, we knew he was going to be under scrutiny because he hadn't had much success with the ball in any form of the game throughout the summer. He's a good performer and friend, but when the opportunity came to get after him on a good wicket at Old Trafford, I'd taken it.

Cricket fever had now become cricket mania, but I was a little disappointed that the newspapers didn't seem to be getting behind us as much as the public. We had just played two great Test matches yet the scribes or their bosses seemed to be more interested in the England players who were pulling out of the C&G semi-finals in order to rest before the Fourth Test at Trent Bridge. How silly it would have looked if, for example, Flintoff and myself had played in the semi-finals and picked up injuries which kept us out of the Test. If we lost Freddie Flintoff in a county game then our Ashes hopes could have gone. Fletcher did not want to leave anything to chance and looking after Fred was one of the main priorities.

We wanted to look after Team England in a selfish kind of way, stating that the only thing which really mattered to us during the summer was the Ashes. We had to make sure our players were fit mentally and physically and we felt the rest and time away from the game would suit them more than travelling to play in a semi-final. It's unfortunate for the counties and I feel for them, but this summer more than any other the international team had to come first, second and third.

Going into Trent Bridge, I wouldn't have said we really had an edge over the Aussies, but I knew we were playing really good cricket. The hard thing is to keep doing it week-in, week-out against good teams. You knew at certain times they would be on top, but for the last two Tests they hadn't had many spells like that. We had dominated and that was a huge thing for us to have done. It showed that we had come on a huge distance as a team.

We really enjoy one another's success, the guys respond to most of the things that are said to them and have worked hard on their games. The discipline of bowling to plans and showing energy in the field had also been taken on board and it certainly made my job a bit easier.

By now, every batsman had runs under his belt, every bowler wickets and each player was feeling good about their game. I felt that as long as the team relaxed between the games and got away from cricket then we would be all right. I played golf with the European Tour's Mark Foster and had one night out with my friends, concentrating on normal things for a week, being Michael Vaughan father, husband and friend rather than Michael Vaughan captain of England. Others did their own thing and when Freddie rang up to say he was going to St Tropez for four days I just said: 'Please do. Get away from it all. Get your feet up and relax and just make sure you arrive next Tuesday ready to go because your workload is going to be massive again.' I wanted us to arrive on the Tuesday a really refreshed cricket team, not stale but wondering how practice was going to go. When you're in that mindset you work better and focus on the little, basic things which are so important.

The practice sessions on the Tuesday and Wednesday went really well and players were focused on the job in hand. We didn't do too much, just enough to make sure we were prepared for the big game.

I will admit that the summer was the hardest I have ever known in my professional life. It really tested my batting and captaincy, mentally and physically. I had to think all the time on the pitch against Australia. To captain well against them you have to be really forward thinking and have your eye five or even 10 overs ahead of the game, making sure you have the right fields to different batsmen, working out how you are going to remove them, how you're going to dry up the runs, how and when to use the sweepers and ensure the opposition don't have many opportunities to score fours. It is a very draining job.

Sometimes you get on a wicket where the best-laid plans are rendered useless, so you have to come up with Plan B very quickly, but if it was easy to captain against the best team in the world then everybody would do it. It certainly taxed my brain and the word 'frazzled' comes to mind.

It's very difficult to appraise yourself as a captain and all I will say is that I was very lucky throughout the summer – and indeed beforehand – to have a very good set of players to work with. They seem to respond to what Duncan Fletcher and I say and you can't ask for much more. I really only ask them for hard work and effort and togetherness, as a team. You only have to see how we react when a wicket goes down to see how together we are. The players really do buy into the team ethic and everybody's attitude has impressed me. Sometimes it can take a while, but this set of lads bonded quickly and that is a very big thing.

I knew the Ashes summer would be the biggest test of my captaincy. People wondered if I could change the course of a game with a few decisions, but even if you do that you still need your bowlers to put the ball in the right areas. They had done that, while the batsmen scored 400 or more in the first innings for each of the middle three Tests against Australia and that takes some doing.

We felt that Trent Bridge would be a good toss to win and for the second successive time I did. Batting first on a good track allows you to put a healthy score on the board although this time we would be facing an unknown force. McGrath succumbed to an elbow problem which brought Kasprowicz back into the series while the Aussies decided to leave out Gillespie and give a debut to young Shaun Tait. We knew he was quick with a slingy action, but that was about it.

We felt their more inexperienced attack might work to our advantage and so it proved as Strauss and Trescothick put together a century partnership in next to no time. There were still only 21 overs bowled when the former was the first to perish, in the most unusual of circumstances. He bottom-edged an attempted sweep off Warne on to his boot and the ball ballooned to Hayden at slip.

Trescothick became Tait's first Test victim when a jaffa of an inswinger went through the gate and into the stumps, and when Bell became the youngster's second, we were 146 for three and suffering a mini collapse. I felt in good touch again and, with Pietersen, steered us to a more respectable position before I suffered the embarrassment of falling to my opposite number. Ponting rarely turns his arm over, but for a period he wobbled the ball in the air and was the most difficult to face. On that surface he was tricky and I'd rather have been at the other end facing Lee, but even so I shouldn't have got out to him. It was a stop-start day because of rain and that never helps batsmen because they repeatedly have to play themselves back in, but there was nothing we could do about the elements.

Honours were probably about even when Pietersen, who has been a breath of fresh air in the dressing room and seems totally undaunted by anything he faces, became the fifth wicket to fall when he edged Lee to Gilchrist, but what followed was arguably the stand of the series to date. It doesn't matter how much criticism Geraint Jones comes in for, he always bounces back and he was a superb partner for the irrepressible Flintoff. Jones has huge mental strength and over the last couple of years he has brought energy to the team both in his play and his attitude on and off the pitch. He knew he'd missed opportunities and should have taken some of them, but a lot of chances had gone down on both sides. Maybe it was just the pressure of people knowing that this was a really tough series and that every chance could be crucial.

What more can be said of Jones's partner Flintoff? He is simply a colossus, an exceptional cricketer, but one thing he is going to have to be a little wary of is our country's tendency to build people up to knock them down. He is strong enough to know and deal with that. He had been a phenomenon throughout the summer: I certainly didn't expect the level of performance that he produced and I doubt that he did either. He had clearly laid down his credentials for Sports Personality of the Year. The pair put on 177 for the sixth wicket, Flintoff once again showing just how accomplished a batsman he has become with 102 while Jones fell just 15 short of a deserved century. We had 477 runs when our innings ended and felt very comfortable.

Now was our chance to really turn the screw and I couldn't have been more delighted that it was Hoggard who started their troubles. There had been a lot of talk about his position in the team – not from within it, however – but when he gets the conditions there are few finer swing bowlers. Trent Bridge was always going to suit his style of bowling and so it proved as he trapped Hayden lbw and later had a very determined Langer taken at short leg. Simon Jones chipped in with the first of his five when he had Ponting straight in front and then Hoggy trapped Martyn in similar fashion. They were rocking and we finally rolled them over for 218: for the first time in nearly two decades they had been asked to follow on.

Before I enforced it, I got all the players together and asked the bowlers if they were strong and willing enough to do it all again and they gave me the right response. 'Let's stick 'em back in and who knows, we might win it today,' was the collective reply. They went back in, but our luck turned when, inside the first 10 overs, Simon Jones went down and it looked like we were reduced to four bowlers for the rest of the match when it was still a good wicket. It didn't swing as much second time round and I knew that it was always going to be harder bowling them out a second time after a follow-on.

But I was impressed by the side's work ethic. We really had to call on all our resources to try to restrict them and ensure we were not having to chase too many. We got wickets at crucial times although when Langer and Ponting were going well I wondered just how difficult it was going to be for us. And then our sub Gary Pratt came on and produced a magnificent piece of fielding to run out Ponting. To say Ponting was not amused was putting it lightly and for all those willing to listen he gave vent to his feelings in no uncertain manner – his tirade costing him three-quarters of his match fee. He had not liked our use of the substitute fielder throughout the series, but he had chosen an inappropriate time to have a rant because Simon Jones was on his way to hospital for a scan when Ponting was run out – and surely he didn't expect us to field with just 10 players. His general complaint was about our bowlers going off too often, but these days they take a lot of fluid on board and every now and again they need a toilet break or to change a hot, sweaty shirt. It's something he had not been happy about, but we were not doing anything outside the laws of the game. There was nothing untoward about it and it wasn't just us. Brad Hodge had fielded for almost the entire match at Old Trafford for Michael Clarke, but we didn't complain even when Hodge took two brilliant catches.

That run-out changed the course of their innings and we finally restricted them to 387, a lead of 128. We knew we were just one partnership away from going ahead in the series, and did not think it would get quite so close before we finally reached our objective. Sometimes those small targets are trickier than bigger ones because you go out and try to finish it early. Then suddenly a couple of wickets fall and a few doubts set in. If you're chasing 220 you bat time and play for your wicket.

Trescothick and Strauss definitely looked as if they wanted to get it over quickly and they had 32 on the board in five overs, but when the former went he was quickly followed by three more and, at 57 for four, people were anxiously starting to look at the scoreboard or wonder if Simon Jones would be able to bat if needed.

The Aussie bowlers also knew that they would not be out there for too long so they ran in that bit harder. They could give it everything for one session because they knew, one way or the other, there wasn't going to be a second. They got wickets, Lee and Warne the main protagonists and for a while the English dressing room was very tense. I'm sure a lot of the players were thinking 'Surely not'. I was never quite so worried, but I definitely did not want everything to come unstuck because I knew how much hard work the players had put into getting us a wonderful position not just in terms of the match, but also the series. I was feeling for them, particularly the bowlers who had given such sterling effort throughout.

Flintoff and Pietersen steadied us, but we were six down with still another 18 wanted. We were still 13 short when the last of our recognised batsmen succumbed. Step forward Ashley Giles and Matthew Hoggard to get us over the line in heart-stopping fashion. Everybody there could see what it meant for us to go 2–1 up by the celebrations that followed the winning runs.

It was already a huge achievement for us to be in that position and I don't think anybody, not even Australians, could have said that we didn't deserve to be where we were, especially after we'd gone 1–0 down at Lord's. I knew we would still have to produce another fantastic performance at The Oval to win back the Ashes, but even if we didn't, and Australia came back to force a win and retain them, then we had still performed heroically. I was convinced, whatever the result, it was going to be another epic.

I was really proud of what the team had already achieved and how the nation responded. You can never win over some critics, but we couldn't have cared less. Cricket was huge and the Ashes were now within touching distance again. The players and management – everybody connected with Team England – had done a magnificent job getting us to where we were. People talk about skills and technique, but a lot of the game is about mentality and our backroom staff had certainly done their job in that respect. I generally don't talk technique at all to the players unless they ask for my advice specifically, but I do work very hard on their mental approach.

There was just one thing left for the summer of 2005. We needed to take one step more when the last match came round at The Oval.

24

COMETH THE HOUR

We got over the line at Trent Bridge and then we had a few rituals to perform, including press conferences and having a few beers in the dressing room with the Aussies. But first one of our latest practices had to be performed – a huddle and a rendition of our team song (which I'm not allowed to divulge but it is about a passion for cricket and was written and brought in by Matthew Maynard, our assistant coach).

By this time, the Aussies were regular after-match visitors. A good spirit had developed between the two sides no matter how fiercely competitive we were on the pitch. That's exactly as it should be – intense but enjoyable rivalry on the pitch and burgeoning friendships off it.

It was 10.15pm before we left the ground and we were a happy bunch, but far from complacent. To have gone 2–1 ahead knowing that the series had captured the hearts and imaginations of the nation was a very gratifying feeling. There were times when I felt like Brad Pitt.

England sides have never had any difficulty at all celebrating a win and we painted Nottingham red, white and blue. To be ahead in the series with just one match to go was indeed just cause for a serious party and as Nelson in Trafalgar Square would testify later, we have some serious party animals in our midst. And why not, as long as it doesn't get out of hand or affect our performance on the pitch.

It was a joy to be home for a day with Nichola and the family, the return to normality I always enjoy. Cricket was not too far away though because it was my testimonial game at Headingley on the Wednesday – a 20-over game between an England side and Yorkshire. I'd got the call after Trent Bridge to say that it was sold out which was incredible considering that at the beginning of the summer we were looking at closer to 5,000 spectators than 20,000.

To get a full house was amazing although I'm enough of a realist to understand that it wasn't me they were particularly coming to see, but the new heroes of English cricket. My testimonial was the fans' excuse to be with the team. It meant a lot to me that they were there and also that players were prepared to travel the length and breadth of the country to support me. Unfortunately horrific thunderstorms meant that not a ball was bowled. It was disappointing because I'm sure the fans would have created a great atmosphere in a bid to give the team a boost before the final game of a series which was already being billed as the best ever.

My original intention had been to open the England innings in what was a carnival match with Giles and Hoggard, the pair who combined to win us the match at Trent Bridge. But then I had second thoughts. If we had already won the Ashes I would have done it, but they were still in the balance and I realised that doing things like that is almost tempting fate and might be looked on as a celebration when we were still a long way from champagne time. I didn't want anything to be thrown back at us and I certainly didn't want to do anything that might act as a motivation for the Aussies. They had unintentionally motivated us and I did not want to do anything that would return the favour.

We were so close now and I sat back reflecting on what had already been the most intense and stressful sporting summer of my life. I knew that every ounce of energy and thought had to go into how we were going to beat the Aussies. Winning back the Ashes was still going to require a monumental effort from team and management.

We had a week off and didn't play for our counties because we wanted to get away from it all for a short while to ensure we arrived in the capital refreshed in body and mind. It was the right approach, but even though I was at home, I was still thinking just cricket, cricket, cricket.

I was totally absorbed by only one thing, winning back that little urn. I didn't spend one hour of any day without thinking about who we were going to pick, how we were going to play the five most important days of our cricketing lives to date. Would I win the toss? How would we play the genius of Warne? Would McGrath produce the kind of spell that rocked us at Lord's in the only match we had lost? Could I get another hundred? What would happen if, if, if . . . They were a few of a million questions swimming through my head.

They were different questions, but it had been the same throughout the summer. My head was spinning all the time I wasn't playing and when I was it had to be nothing less than 100% concentration.

I was probably a nightmare to live with, as Nichola would most likely testify. My conversation was very limited and unless it was cricket all other images were blurred. If somebody asked me a question, I'd try to give them an answer, but my concentration was elsewhere. My mind had been invaded by the deep desire to win back Test cricket's greatest prize.

I remember going out in Sheffield with a few friends about 10 days before the Fourth Test at Trent Bridge. Nobody enjoys a good laugh more than me and my next all-night party will not be the first, but on this occasion I just went home at 10pm because my mind was purely focused on cricket and I offered not one thing to the night out. I was a nightmare for friends and family. I just felt that nothing had to come between me and my desire to beat the Aussies. It was stressful and I'm sure I was a pain in the neck to those around me, but you get nothing without hard work and my job was far from over. The party could wait.

Nichola offered not one word of complaint throughout what must have been an ordeal for her as well. She's simply the best because by this time she was carrying our second child. She understood how difficult it was for me to switch off because everybody was asking about it. People were beginning to recognise me more and wanted to know more about me and the game and the team. I was asked about every single aspect and situation which the Fourth Test had brought up. Cricket took over my life. The nation was becoming similarly gripped with Ashes Fever.

There was one pleasant diversion before we met up at The Oval, when I was involved in a golf day at Sunningdale. It was a nice, relaxing way to take my mind off things and our team finished second. I was hoping it was not an omen. My thoughts were not allowed to stray from cricket for long. Everybody was still asking about the Ashes and I did a few interviews. I had to present the third-place prize to Sam Torrance and I received a tremendous ovation when I went up. It didn't matter who they were: celebrities from other spheres, grandmas, Old Uncle Tom Cobleigh – everybody was excited about the week ahead. Sam had won the Ryder Cup as captain and he wished me all the best in our quest for glory. I so wanted to experience what he had – lifting the ultimate trophy. There were many celebrities there and they were asking if we'd play Collingwood or Jimmy Anderson, how was the team going to react to the pressure, what was the weather forecast, would it rain for three days. It was Cricket Fever and everybody was affected.

I enjoy meeting people from other sports – Lawrence Dallaglio, Matt Dawson, Keith Wood, Zinzan Brooke, Kenny Dalglish and Alan Hansen were among those there – to assess their mentality and what it means to be part of something massive in the country's consciousness. I know what I'm like when the big football's on or rugby or Tim Henman, I'm always right behind them. Here I was trying to work out what went on in their heads when the heat of the conflict was at its most intense.

And so to The Oval. The team arrived very fresh in body, although you could sense there was a bit more pressure around the squad. It was understandable given what was at stake and how much it meant to so many people. Not only that, but the team had worked very hard to get into the position they were in. A lot of the guys were asking questions of themselves. They knew it was still going to take a colossal effort, but they did not want to fall at the final hurdle.

Losing Simon Jones to injury was a huge blow given the way he had bowled throughout the summer, but it was a position which we could not dwell on. The question of who would replace him came down to a choice between the Lancashire paceman Anderson or the Durham all-rounder Collingwood. We were of the opinion that it wouldn't swing too much so we bolstered our batting and fielding by including Collingwood. We wanted his all-round game not just his batting. He could bowl a few overs if necessary and there are few better fielders in the game – if any. With Colly coming in at No. 7 it looked a formidable line-up. The Aussies had to get 20 wickets and weather forecasts for Friday and Saturday were not very bright, particularly if you were Australian and needing the maximum amount of time.

I think we all felt that it was always going to come down to how well we could bat against Warne on a pitch that was bound to suit him eventually. As it turned out, it suited him from the off. There again, he could get a ball to jump up and turn out of porridge.

The toss was going to be crucial although the way the weather went it didn't influence the outcome as it might have done. However, winning it did create a positive edge for the team and you could sense there was a collective relief that we had first chance to impose ourselves on them and the match.

I always speak to the team the day before a game, though on Wednesday I didn't talk for as long as I had when we were 1–0 down going into Edgbaston. I told them just to ensure they expressed themselves, to go out and play as normally as they could. I didn't want the fact that we only needed a draw to affect the way we approached and played the game. I wanted us to express ourselves as if it had been 1–1 and we needed to win. We had to take them on and play in the most positive manner, whether we were batting or bowling, and to make sure our body language was very good at all times. The players appreciated that, but it was still difficult to get away from the knowledge that we only needed a draw and the Ashes would be coming home. The prospect of rain did not fill our hearts with dread. I was not alone in that feeling – everybody in the dressing room and those watching live or on television were of a similar mind.

There was another side of me that wanted to beat them and win 3–1, but I was prepared to settle for anything as long as it meant we were still ahead when the bails came off for the last time.

It was difficult not to get caught up in the emotion of the occasion because the crowd went ballistic at anything positive we did and there was a collective silence when anything negative occurred. You can get lured into playing for the applause and big roars which greeted every England run or Australian wicket: we had to stay focused on the game as it developed, not on the prize. The matches throughout the summer had changed so fast that I knew if we lost our concentration the game could slip away within an hour. We had to live by the cliché of one ball at a time.

We got off to the perfect start, but they have a genius in Warne and he was about to weave one of his spells. With the possible exception of Sri Lanka's Muttiah Muralitharan, no other bowler in the world could have got out of that first-day Oval pitch what Warne did. Against any other team we would have been 350 for three at the close on a strip that was easy paced with no bounce, swing or seam. Unfortunately it did have spin and they had Warne – a lethal cocktail and so it proved as he took six wickets.

We were 82 without loss and looking good, then 131 for

four and not looking good at all, but I had lost count of how many times Flintoff held his hand up throughout the series, and here he was again sharing in a partnership of 143 with the impressive Strauss. Not for the first time, our tail wagged and we reached a reasonably respectable 373, although I knew it was not a total that had put Australia out of the game. We were, I felt, between 80 and 100 below par.

We had controlled a lot of their players very well. Hayden, Gilchrist, Martyn, Katich and Clarke had not really hurt us too much, but we knew the wicket was made for somebody to produce a big score. Unfortunately two of them did and they were both openers.

Australia were 185 before their first wicket went down and Hayden grinded for every one of his runs. He had not been able to bully us as he had so many teams the world over, but here he would prove a threat to our ambition. Both he and Langer amassed centuries but, given the likely weather, I still felt that whatever they scored we would need to bat 80 or 90 overs in our second innings to make the game safe.

What I hadn't bargained for was that we would actually go in second time round with a lead, albeit a slender one. What contributed to that was Australia taking the light on the Friday evening when there were still plenty of overs to go. Hayden and Langer had us at their mercy at that point and I was facing the prospect of having to find a few more bowlers, myself included, to get us through the day. They saved us that worry. I was relieved when they went off, not to mention more than a little surprised, given that they needed as much time as they could get. For them a win would square the series and retain the Ashes: no other result was good enough.

Being offered the light is a tricky situation and it is always difficult to know what to do for the best. Hindsight's a wonderful thing, but they probably felt afterwards that they should have stayed out there on the Friday evening. It looked like they missed an opportunity, but there were no complaints from us, just a few raised eyebrows.

A lot of time was lost to rain on the Saturday, but it didn't seem to matter to those who had paid to watch cricket. The umbrellas went up and they were singing in the rain. It didn't look much better on the Sunday, a miserable, drizzly grey day. The players in the outfield couldn't see the ball, but when we took the new one it started to swing. Freddie bowled the spell of the summer and put them under so much pressure as he moved the ball around. Hoggard also produced a wonderful spell. The Sunday morning was a present from the cricketing gods: to wake up and have those conditions was our reward for all the hard work we had put in during the summer. I had expected them to get 550 and for us to have to bat for 100 overs, but to have them out for less than our 373 was incredible. If they had got 200 ahead it would have been very difficult for us knowing that we were just batting for a draw, but to be ahead meant that every one of our runs counted twice because for every one of ours they had to cancel it out. That was massive.

We took our chance and Freddie was unbelievable. He just wouldn't come off. I couldn't get the ball out of his hands. I kept on saying: 'Just one more, Fred' and he'd reply: 'No way. I'm fine. I'm going through the whole session.' I think he sniffed a five-for and that was his due reward. I just can't imagine what it's like for him, running in as he does, pounding down his legs time after time. It was also great to see Hoggard getting his rewards, for he gets some criticism (not from within the dressing room I may add and neither does Geraint Jones or anybody else for that matter) but when the conditions suit him there are few better. Our togetherness and support for one another is a strong element of our side. If anybody sees another player getting a rough time from outside the team then they always rally round. We build one another up and let everybody know just how valuable they are to the team.

I'd personally been disappointed that I hadn't got another hundred after Old Trafford. I had never felt more relaxed and in control than when I went out to bat on the Monday at The Oval. A positive approach was going to be important because I knew scoring runs was going to be just as vital as batting overs. We had to make sure we got as far ahead of them as possible.

My intention was to show the team that was the approach we wanted and I was feeling good when McGrath bowled me another beauty. But then that's what he does; you hold your hand up and walk off. Next ball Ian Bell got another from him and he was walking back too.

I know one thing after this wonderful, nerve-jangling summer: it is far easier batting in the middle than watching from the dressing room. When I'm on the pitch, I feel very controlled and calm, but when I'm in the dressing room watching, it becomes a lot more stressful. I couldn't let it show just how much it was getting to me when Pietersen tried to swish Warne out of the ground and missed or somebody chased a wide one. I can't show anything, but I'll admit that deep down it's killing me.

Warne was always going to be a massive factor, but I felt

that we still had a chance to win the game if we could set them anything around 250. Even if we were only 150 ahead I knew it would be a difficult chase.

But cometh the hour, cometh Kevin Pietersen. The way he played and his whole temperament and approach was perfect. He took them on. Before lunch he had taken a battering from Lee, who was bowling as fast as he had all summer. Pietersen survived and at lunch I told him not to alter his approach, but to look to score and not just survive. His game is naturally aggressive and I reminded him of that. His response was magnificent.

I think the few overs after lunch when he was hitting Lee into the stands was the time when the Aussies realised the Ashes were gone. To make 158 in those circumstances was a superb effort, but there were heroes elsewhere and everywhere. Giles hit a career best and I think everybody in the dressing room celebrated that as much as they did Pietersen's century, while Collingwood made the best 10 of his life, off 51 balls. The runs were mounting, the overs were running out and when we were 250 ahead I knew the Ashes were coming home.

Team spirit is created by winning, but if you have a mentality of enjoying your cricket and getting together as a unit, training hard together and making sure the management's philosophy is exactly the same – and there's certainly no 'them and us' with our management – then it is easier to develop. Management are just as important as players in my eyes and we make sure they are involved with us all the time. Freddie's an incredible cricketer and I'm the captain, but we have an environment where nobody is on a pedestal and nobody looks up to anybody else. Ian Bell is the youngest player in the team, but I encourage him to feel that he is just as important as me or anybody else.

Out on the pitch, the job was all but over and both teams knew when our innings ended that so had their interest in the series. The little urn was ours and Ponting was particularly gracious in defeat. Before Australia went out again, we met behind the dressing rooms with the match referee and all decided it was time for a bit of common sense. We did have to return to the pitch, but three balls later the umpires offered the light and the Aussie batsmen took it. All that was left after we went off was for the umpires to go back out and take off the bails to signal the end of 16 years of Australian domination.

Ponting said to me that we had been the better team, had played the better cricket and fully deserved our success. They were all obviously gutted because they really had not believed that we could beat them. They had such self-belief and confidence, and they thought they could batter us. Well, the fish of England refused to be fried.

They had contributed to their own downfall, however. When Glenn McGrath said he felt Australia would win 5–0 all our players looked at his words and used them as a huge motivational tool. We knew we were not a team who would be beaten 5–0 and if he thought we were then we would show him otherwise.

When you face Australia as player or coach you get tested to the ultimate level and we survived the examination with our heads high, our chests out and our reputation as a team enhanced. Nothing in our sporting lives had felt better.

Looking back, I think people will consider the 2005 Ashes series as the greatest ever. They will say that the England team had a huge amount of self-belief and showed an enormous amount of character – and then they will look at Shane Warne and say: 'How the hell did he finish on the losing team?' He took 40 wickets, scored nearly 250 runs and finished on the losing team. It's almost unbelievable.

Will there ever be a series that's played in the same spirit? Will there ever be a series where it never stops ebbing and flowing? Will there ever be a series that grips the nation? Will women and grannies ever get hooked by cricket again? Will any man ever take 40 wickets again and finish on the losing side? I doubt it.

This was a freak of a series. The cricket that was played, the manner in which everything happened was unique. There was some incredible batting, magnificent bowling, one-handed catches. If there was anything missing from that series, I would like to know what it was because I wasn't aware of anything. It had absolutely everything.

Our support was magnificent and the Aussies received plenty of stick. The Barmy Army sang: 'Stand-up if you're 2–1 up' and when Glenn McGrath showed with his fingers that he thought the series would finish 2–2, they replied with: 'Sit down if you're 2–1 down' . . . and McGrath entered into the spirit of things by sitting on the boundary rope.

Our crowd certainly deserved a lot of credit for the way they got behind us and put them under a lot of pressure every time they fielded the ball. The Aussies took it well, they were humorous and they all came out with dark glasses in the gloom on the Sunday, a light-hearted attempt to persuade the umpires that the light was good enough for play to continue.

I had already learned before the series started that the captain comes under immense scrutiny. People constantly look to see the way you work, the way you respond to different situations and the environment you create. They look at your tactics and your batting, how you speak to your players and the media, the way you do absolutely everything. But when you play Australia it goes to a whole new level. The focus is 10 times as intense. There had been a lot of talk about the importance of the captaincy, but I had not expected anything like this scrutiny.

Looking back now I realise just what a good decision I took before the series when I decided not to look at much that was written, be it complimentary or critical. I didn't want my thinking to be confused in any way. I wanted to make sure that my mind was completely focused on what I wanted to do, and not what the critics wanted me to do. Sometimes you can read articles and, whether or not you agree, it can affect the way you think. You start querying your decisions and I just wanted to do things my way. I wanted to ensure I failed or succeeded doing it my way. I wasn't going to be bullied into doing it another way and I think that was crucial.

As for the captaincy, I'm sure the debate will continue about whether it has affected my batting, but I will stay on as long as England want me. We are a team and as long as the management think that I am the man to carry the side forward, then I will. The team is the most important thing, not the individuals, and I have no goals about winning a certain number of games or series other than aiming to win as many as possible.

Some might say: 'Winning The Ashes? Can it get any better?' Well it might. There's a huge opportunity for us to go to Australia to retain them and I would like to have the chance to take the team down there in a bid to do it. And then there's the World Cup after that. Who knows? As long as the team is together and responding, and the environment we create is the right one, then I would love to go on as long as I can. That's out of my hands. What I do have in them at the moment, however, are the Ashes.

I don't think we are the best team in the world, but we can be and we are definitely one of the most exciting sides to watch, have been for a long time. Something always seems to happen and in the summer of 2005 it did, something very, very special.

We must kick on now and make sure the awareness of cricket we have rekindled becomes a huge bonfire of interest, with kids who want to play getting the opportunity. I want cricket to be popular not just because of the Ashes but because of what is being achieved in six months' time, a year's time, two years and so on.

Until we went on that unbelievable open-top bus ride through London I had no idea whatsoever about how much it mattered and meant to so many people. And if I had known, it might have frightened me. Seeing the happiness on the faces in the streets was as good a moment for me as standing on that stage and lifting the Ashes. We made people happy in our country and that's the best feeling of all.

Congratulations poured in from the moment we won. The Queen described the series as 'truly memorable' and our success as a 'magnificent achievement'. Her Majesty added: 'Both sides can take credit for giving us all such a wonderfully exciting and entertaining summer of cricket at its best.'

Tony Blair, David Beckham and the England football team, Sir Elton John, Mick Jagger and The Stones, Ian Woosnam,

John Major, Silverdale School back home in Sheffield: many, many messages came through from all over the world, together with those from England players of the past. It meant a lot, not just to the players who did it, but to those who hadn't been successful. They'd tried as hard as we did and got battered and had been through the pain of being beaten and belittled by the Aussies. They were genuinely happy for us. We were just the lucky XI to do it this time.

The world rankings don't occupy too much of our attention, because we just look to be competitive in every series that we play. Australia have been winning home and away for a number of years, and our side have yet to win on the subcontinent, so comparisons are not yet realistic.

This was our sixth Series victory on the bounce so I must have done something right.

Postscript

Our tour to Pakistan was never going to be easy just because we'd won the Ashes. Win, lose or draw beforehand, it makes no difference – Pakistan's always going to be difficult.

People blamed our defeat there on us losing focus after beating the Australians. I didn't go along with that at all. The only thing that was different was that our profile had risen and our diaries were busier. All those involved in the Ashes triumph deserved to celebrate to the full, but I had no doubts that by late October we were completely ready for what would face us both on and off the pitch.

For four and a half days of the First Test we played as well as we had at any time against Australia. We should have won. Unfortunately a rush of blood while chasing a highly gettable target of 198 cost us dear, and also gave the Pakistanis an unexpected boost – particularly their best bowler Shoaib Akhtar and their captain Inzamam-ul-Haq. The influence of coach Bob Woolmer also had an obvious effect on the way they played.

We should have won the match and didn't, but it could not be blamed on poor preparation or too much celebration. Instead I give full credit to Pakistan for what happened on that final afternoon and in the next two Tests. Whenever they could put us under pressure they did, especially Shoaib, who bowled fast and as well as he had for many seasons. He was a huge difference between the teams. A constant threat when attacking at speed, he had also perfected a slower ball which we found almost unplayable. Unfortunately we couldn't apply the same amount of pressure to their batsmen. Once we were behind in the series we were always going to struggle – and so it proved.

I couldn't take any part in the First Test because my troublesome knee broke down again in one of the warm-up games. I was running in a straight line when I felt it, and I knew I was never going to make our first serious match since the triumph at The Oval. Instead Marcus Trescothick stood in. He captained well and hit a very big hundred to help set up what should have been a comfortable run chase.

Looking back now, I should have come home and got everything sorted when I first knew there was a problem. But having lost that Test I was desperate to play in the others. To be honest, I wasn't at my best physically and was being treated before play and after play, as well as during lunch and tea. I wanted to help so much, but staying on perhaps hindered my recovery.

I went home before the one-dayers for keyhole surgery, which basically cleaned up the knee. Then I faced a couple of months in rehab. My progress seemed good, but a week before flying to India for the second leg of our winter tour I started to feel a few twinges. And when I got there, the problem deteriorated to such an extent that I had to pull out of the match immediately before the First Test. Injections did not provide a cure and eventually I had to come home again. With Marcus already having left for personal reasons, the captaincy was handed to Freddie Flintoff and typically he led from the front, dealing well with the added burden and proving an inspirational figure. A drawn series in India was a great achievement.

I was particularly low when I left because it was the second time in successive tours that I had been forced to return early. I wondered if the problem could be sorted out. I admit that I even started to worry that it could be the end for me as a professional cricketer.

But a few weeks and a course of injections later, I am full of optimism and not pessimistic in the slightest. Everything feels good, the injections are oiling the joint and I am looking forward to a complete recovery and return to the Test arena.

Despite what has been written – most of it rubbish and little of it informed – I am confident of leading England in both forms of the game for the foreseeable future. I believe I still have plenty to offer and won't be giving anything up for as long as I feel England has a better team with me in it.

My recovery is going well and I'm desperate to get back in the middle. I still believe that I have plenty of shots to call.

PLAYER PROFILES
by
Michael Vaughan

Marcus Trescothick

It says everything about the man that Marcus, my chief rival for the captaincy once Nasser Hussain stood down, was the first to call with his congratulations when I got the job. He is the ultimate team player and I could not have wished for a better right-hand man – although he is of course a left-hander.

Marcus gives valuable advice from first slip and is just about as dependable a guy as there is in the dressing room. No praise is high enough for the Somerset opener and nobody was happier for him than me when he started laying into the Australians during the 2005 Ashes series. He had not previously enjoyed the best of fortune against the world champions, but this time he had worked out a way of playing them and he was rewarded with a stream of runs.

To those who have criticised him for his lack of foot movement, I just say, look in the scorebook. When he hit 100 not out against Bangladesh in June 2005, it was his ninth one-day international century, beating Graham Gooch's previous England record of eight. Marcus reached 5,000 Test runs during the Old Trafford Ashes match, his 64th Test; for England only Hobbs, Hammond, Hutton and Barrington got them faster.

Duncan Fletcher first spotted Marcus's potential when he was Glamorgan coach and within a year of taking over with England, called him up to a role he has filled with distinction. *Wisden Cricketers' Almanack* named him one of their five Cricketers of the Year in 2005 – a richly deserved honour. It would not surprise me in the slightest if Marcus goes on to become England's most capped player.

Australia's first innings goes pear-shaped – Steve Harmison and I are fairly pleased about the wicket of Clarke, out lbw.

A measured response from the England captain on the occasion of England's narrow victory in the Fourth Test.

The impressive Strauss shares a 143 partnership with Flintoff in our first innings at The Oval.

Simon Jones was out of the reckoning for The Oval, so Paul Collingwood was called on.

Left: Australia's Matthew Hayden silences his critics in the final Test.

Below: Cometh the hour, cometh Kevin Pietersen – he sweeps Warne on his way to a Test-turning innings at The Oval.

Great mates with more in common than the ear-rings – Warne and Pietersen symbolise indomitable courage to their respective sides.

Hoggard congratulates Ashley Giles, who constructed a career-best 59 that laid to rest Australia's last hope of saving the Ashes.

Bad light may have stopped play but nothing could dim our victory. I lead the team down the steps at The Oval, 12 September 2005.

And they all sang 'Jerusalem'.

So there you are, Little Urn!

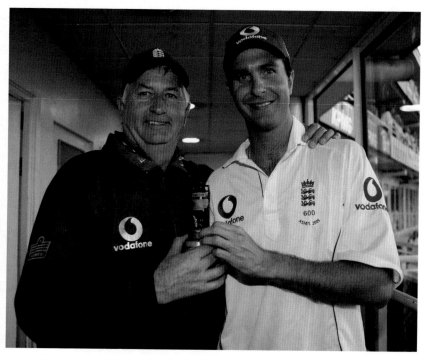

Duncan Fletcher is seen to crack his face as he gets one hand on the Ashes.

You won't get a lot in that – Trescothick, Flintoff and I are ready for a bevy.

Trafalgar Square celebrations – even Nichola and Tallulah look half asleep.

Andrew Strauss

From the moment Andrew stepped into the England dressing room for his Test debut, against New Zealand at Lord's in 2004, he looked as if he belonged. It was not just his century and man-of-the-match award, but the way he spoke and behaved. Called into the England side when I was injured, he might have become an embarrassment to the selectors had Nasser Hussain not decided to retire from international cricket after the match. I think Nasser, who knows a thing or two about the game, saw a more-than-capable replacement and he has been proved right.

Strauss went on to complete a rare double when he hit a ton and was again man of the match in his first overseas Test, later that year against South Africa in Port Elizabeth. It was also in South Africa – the land of his birth, although he was educated at Radley College and Durham University – that he scored his 1,000th Test run in only his 10th match.

Comfortable on front and back foot and one of the most elegant of batsmen, he quickly came to terms with playing Shane Warne after the greatest spinner of all time got one to turn a yard and a half to bowl him at Edgbaston. It was no surprise when he collected his first century against the Aussies later in the 2005 series. Strauss has already captained Middlesex so no doubt his name will be in the frame when I decide to stand down or the selectors decide they have had enough of me. Hopefully there are a lot more runs to come from both of us before then.

Ian Bell

Like Andrew Strauss, Ian looked international calibre as soon as he became part of the England set-up – a promotion he deserved after making a mountain of runs for Warwickshire. I can pay him no greater tribute than to call him a natural cricketer with equal measures of class, fortitude and determination.

Ian has actually been around the England camp for several years despite being only 23 when the Ashes series started. He reached the national Under-19 side two years ahead of schedule and prompted the former England captain Mike Gatting to call him the best prospect he had ever seen at that level. He has done much to justify that sentiment since, and I am convinced that he will remain an England regular for many seasons to come – and having already captained England's A team, who's to say he might not go on to lead the senior side at some stage?

Although he is hardly likely to rank alongside Andrew Flintoff in the all-rounder category, 'Belly' as his friends call him has been known to turn his arm over now and again and he is a more than useful short leg with several victims already to his name.

Those who know more than the captain, coach and selectors, wondered about Ian's place in the team after his start against Australia, but two half-centuries in the Old Trafford Test showed just how valuable he is becoming to this England team. Although not quite as vociferous or demonstrative as some of his colleagues, Ian is already a much-admired and liked member of what became throughout the summer a very closely knit squad.

Kevin Pietersen

There isn't a lot that hasn't already been said about him, even though he has only been in Test cricket two minutes. KP has made that big an impact. The South African-born right-hander not only has an English mother, but also the mother and father of hard-hitting talents. He lacks nothing in courage and confidence and I believe he can go just as far as he wants to with his adopted country, after being frustrated by lack of opportunity in the southern hemisphere.

The England crest is already tattooed on an arm and his haircuts are always something to behold. There is no doubting his patriotism or ability and he literally forced his way into the side on the back of some magnificent one-day innings.

Initially, I wondered if he was just a banger but those doubts were dispelled once I spent a bit of time with him in the middle. As long as we can keep him grounded and he doesn't get too carried away with his celebrity status, then this young man can become one of the very best.

It says much about the man that he performed so magnificently during the 2004–05 one-day series in South Africa. Booed and barracked wherever he went, KP nevertheless hit three centuries including the fastest ever by an England player – 100 off just 69 balls at East London.

Pietersen's arrival hastened Graham Thorpe's international retirement, but he knows he has plenty to do to emulate his illustrious predecessor. I wouldn't back against him making a pretty good fist of it however. Nobody goes for a loo break when he and Freddie Flintoff are at the crease together.

Andrew Flintoff

Freddie, as he is globally known, although he prefers Fred and his wife Rachael is forbidden from calling him anything other than Andrew, is already a hero – and I don't mind admitting that I'm one of his following.

A cricketing colossus, people have long compared him to Ian Botham, but I'm not sure it's fair to judge players of different generations. I'll leave it by saying that I'd certainly like to have had both at my disposal. Both are brilliant match-winners. Freddie is a genuine all-rounder and although he sees himself more as a batsman/bowler, it is not easy to determine which discipline he is better at. Over the last two years he has matured well as a batsman and very well as a bowler.

It's a great comfort for a captain to have somebody of his stature and ability in the side – and not just for his batting and bowling. He is an outstanding slip fielder and also an astute tactician as befits somebody who as a boy represented Lancashire at chess. His observations are always gladly received.

People often asked during the summer of 2005 if I was ever tempted to give Freddie the new ball. I'm sure he would use it well, but he is such a formidable force coming on after 10 or 12 overs that it might be counter-productive and we don't want to burn him out because he is such a valuable member of the side.

Freddie works hard and plays hard and that's fine by me as long as he is ready for action when the call comes. I've never played with a talent like him and I just hope people aren't building him up ready to knock him down. He is nothing less than a national treasure and should be respected as such.

Geraint Jones

Geraint came into the England team in somewhat controversial manner during the 2003–04 winter tour of the West Indies. Chris Read had not done too much wrong as wicketkeeper, but we needed somebody coming in at No. 7 capable of getting a hundred. There were plenty of people in the England camp who identified Geraint as the man most likely to do so.

Geraint didn't get much chance to show his class in that first match because he spent most of his debut watching Brian Lara hit a world-record 400 not out. He subsequently made very valuable contributions during the visits of New Zealand and West Indies in the summer of 2004. He has been invaluable to me while I'm captaining for the steady flow of information coming from behind the stumps and he has already proved himself to have an acute cricket brain.

A few missed chances here and there have brought criticism, but resilience is one of his biggest characteristics and no matter what has been said and written, Geraint always seems to bounce back with the right answer in the middle. A positive influence in the dressing room and a good communicator, Geraint showed awareness and agility to dismiss Michael Kasprowicz and level the Ashes series at Edgbaston.

Ashley Giles

There are no cliques in the England dressing room today, unlike when I first came into it, but players are always going to have those they would consider their close friends. Ash, also known as Gilo or the 'King of Spain' (courtesy of a mis-spelling of 'Spin'), comes into that category.

Ash started his professional cricketing life as a seamer with Surrey, but when he moved to Warwickshire in 1992, his coach Bob Woolmer encouraged him to bowl left-arm spin. It was the making of him as a cricketer and although he does not turn the ball as much as Shane Warne – who does? – he has been a reliable and consistent performer and excellent at bowling to plans – an important art in modern-day cricket.

Ash has repaid England's faith in him and during our record-breaking year of 2004 his contributions were such that he was awarded a place among *Wisden*'s five Cricketers of the Year – fitting for somebody who is one of only 10 Englishmen to take 100 Test wickets and hit 1,000 runs for their country. None of those runs was more important than the ones he scored in partnership with Matthew Hoggard at Trent Bridge, when we were in the middle of a collapse while chasing a low score to take the lead in the Ashes series.

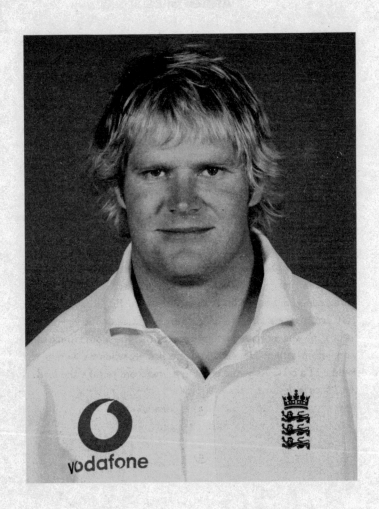

Matthew Hoggard

One of the most resilient and honest of bowlers, Hoggy just keeps running in over after over. He came into the England team during 2000 and quickly proved that his right-arm fast-medium was capable of troubling the world's best batsmen.

Hoggy is already one of the few in history to have taken a hat-trick in a Test match, a feat he achieved when we bowled out West Indies for 94 in their second innings at Barbados during our 2003–04 tour. But it was in South Africa in January 2005, that he really sprang to the nation's attention when he took career-best figures of 12 for 205, England's best since Botham's 13 for 106 against India in 1979–80. My Yorkshire colleague has one of the biggest hearts in the game and has done much to make nonsense of the critics' belief that he can only bowl well in conditions that suit his swing bowling.

England have developed a team ethic over the last few years which has involved nobody giving their wicket away, and no one has worked harder at his batting than Hoggy. Our occasional night-watchman, he has also chipped in with valuable runs at crucial times – most recently at Trent Bridge where he and Giles steered us to victory in a nerve-tingling end to the match.

I was hoping to repay the team's debt to the pair by inviting them to open the innings for the England side facing Yorkshire in a 20-over match for my benefit, but unfortunately the weather intervened.

Stephen Harmison

England have waited a long time for a fast bowler capable of testing batsmen with 90mph deliveries on a regular basis. In Harmy, we have found one. Steve, a 6ft 4in Durham lad, is another good example of what comes through consistency of selection. However, England may have to thank an international from a different code for his elevation to one of the world's best.

After returning injured from the 2003–04 tour of Bangladesh, Harmy went to work on his fitness with his beloved Newcastle United, saw just how hard Alan Shearer worked at staying in shape and decided he'd better do the same. The effects were to be seen in the West Indies when at some points in the series I was able to employ just about everybody to crowd the bat. It wasn't that I was showing off or being over-aggressive, just that I couldn't see the ball going anywhere else but the slip cordon. He took seven for 12 in Jamaica as West Indies were skittled for 47, their lowest-ever Test total.

Harmy is an uncomplicated character, although he is quite open about how homesick he gets on long tours and is never happier than when at home in the north-east. But there isn't a captain in the world who would not want a Harmison firing on all cylinders in his side. He is that good – you don't get to the top of the world rankings if you aren't – and I prefer watching him from the bowler's end to facing him.

Simon Jones

I have been excited by Simon's presence in the England camp ever since he first set foot in the dressing room for his debut against India in 2002. Genuinely quick, he had the happy knack of making a breakthrough every time the ball was thrown to him. There was always a feeling that something was going to happen.

Unfortunately, when sliding to stop a boundary during the first morning of the 2002–03 Ashes series, Simon ruptured an anterior cruciate ligament and was out of Test cricket until the tour to the Caribbean a year later. His fortitude was shown in the way he fought back from that nasty injury and into the side. Some believe that he is an even better bowler now. The Aussies didn't discover much about him on our 2002–03 tour, but they have since and he was a leading wicket-taker in the 2005 Ashes series before injury forced him out of the final Test.

I have no doubt that Simon will develop into one of the world's best fast bowlers, particularly now that he can move the ball both ways and is a master of reverse-swing. What's more I expect him to claw his way up the batting order for he already has an average of more than 15 which isn't bad at all for a No. 11.

Paul Collingwood

Colly is always one of the first names on the one-day teamsheet, but he has had much greater difficulty forcing his way into the full Test side. It reflects the strength England have that he has had so few opportunities. A brilliant fielder, technically sound batsman and useful medium-pacer, he is an all-round cricketer and extremely enthusiastic. His sharp cricket brain makes him a captain's dream and he has the ability to adapt to any situation. It says much about how highly he is thought of that when Simon Jones failed a fitness test for the final 2005 Ashes Test at The Oval, Colly was drafted into the side. It was the first and only change of the entire series.

MICHAEL VAUGHAN'S RESULTS
AS CAPTAIN OF ENGLAND

Compiled by Vic Isaacs

TEST MATCHES

1	England v South Africa	Lord's	31 July 2003	Lost by innings and 92 runs
2	England v South Africa	Trent Bridge	14 August 2003	Won by 70 runs
3	England v South Africa	Headingley	21 August 2003	Lost by 191 runs
4	England v South Africa	The Oval	04 September 2003	Won by 8 wickets

Series: England 2 South Africa 2 Drawn 1
(Nasser Hussain captained England in the drawn first match of the series at Edgbaston)

5	England v Bangladesh	Dhaka	21 October 2003	Won by 7 wickets
6	England v Bangladesh	Chittagong	29 October 2003	Won by 329 runs

Series: England 2 Bangladesh 0

7	England v Sri Lanka	Galle	02 December 2003	Drawn
8	England v Sri Lanka	Kandy	10 December 2003	Drawn
9	England v Sri Lanka	SSC, Colombo	18 December 2003	Lost by innings and 215 runs

Series: England 0 Sri Lanka 1 Drawn 2

10	England v West Indies	Jamaica	11 March 2004	Won by 10 wickets
11	England v West Indies	Trinidad	19 March 2004	Won by 7 wickets
12	England v West Indies	Barbados	01 April 2004	Won by 8 wickets
13	England v West Indies	Antigua	10 April 2004	Drawn

Series: England 3 West Indies 0 Drawn 1

14	England v New Zealand	Headingley	03 June 2004	Won by 9 wickets
15	England v New Zealand	Trent Bridge	10 June 2004	Won by 4 wickets

Series: England 3 New Zealand 0 (Michael Vaughan was injured and did not play in the first Test at Lord's)

16	England v West Indies	Lord's	22 July 2004	Won by 210 runs
17	England v West Indies	Edgbaston	29 July 2004	Won by 256 runs
18	England v West Indies	Old Trafford	12 August 2004	Won by 7 wickets
19	England v West Indies	The Oval	19 August 2004	Won by 10 wickets
	Series: England 4 West Indies 0			
20	England v South Africa	Port Elizabeth	17 December 2004	Won by 7 wickets
21	England v South Africa	Durban	26 December 2004	Drawn
22	England v South Africa	Cape Town	02 January 2005	Lost by 196 runs
23	England v South Africa	Johannesburg	13 January 2005	Won by 77 runs
24	England v South Africa	Centurion	21 January 2005	Drawn
	Series: England 2 South Africa 1 Drawn 2			
25	England v Bangladesh	Lord's	26 May 2005	Won by innings and 239 runs
26	England v Bangladesh	Riverside	03 June 2005	Won by innings and 27 runs
	Series: England 2 Bangladesh 0			
27	England v Australia	Lord's	21 July 2005	Lost by 239 runs
28	England v Australia	Edgbaston	04 August 2005	Won by 2 runs
29	England v Australia	Old Trafford	11 August 2005	Drawn
30	England v Australia	Trent Bridge	25 August 2005	Won by 3 wickets
31	England v Australia	The Oval	08 September 2005	Drawn
	Series: England 2 Australia 1 Drawn 2			

ONE-DAY INTERNATIONALS

17 June 2003	NWB Challenge 2003	England v Pakistan	Old Trafford	Lost by 2 wickets
20 June 2003	NWB Challenge 2003	England v Pakistan	The Oval	Won by 7 wickets
22 June 2003	NWB Challenge 2003	England v Pakistan	Lord's	Won by 4 wickets

Series: England 2 Pakistan 1

26 June 2003	NWB Series 2003	England v Zimbabwe	Trent Bridge	Lost by 4 wickets
01 July 2003	NWB Series 2003	England v Zimbabwe	Headingley	No result
03 July 2003	NWB Series 2003	England v South Africa	Old Trafford	Lost by 7 wickets
06 July 2003	NWB Series 2003	England v Zimbabwe	Bristol	Won by 6 wickets
08 July 2003	NWB Series 2003	England v South Africa	Edgbaston	Won by 4 wickets
12 July 2003	NWB Series 2003	England v South Africa	Lord's	Won by 7 wickets

Series: England won

07 November 2003	England in Bangladesh 2003–04	Bangladesh v England	Chittagong	Won by 7 wickets
10 November 2003	England in Bangladesh 2003–04	Bangladesh v England	Dhaka	Won by 7 wickets
12 November 2003	England in Bangladesh 2003–04	Bangladesh v England	Dhaka	Won by 7 wickets

Series: England 3 Bangladesh 0

| 18 November 2003 | England in Sri Lanka 2003–04 | Sri Lanka v England | Dambulla | Lost by 10 wickets |

Series: England 0 Sri Lanka 1

18 April 2004	England in West Indies 2003–04	West Indies v England	Georgetown	Won by 2 wickets
24 April 2004	England in West Indies 2003–04	West Indies v England	Port of Spain	No result
01 May 2004	England in West Indies 2003–04	West Indies v England	St Lucia	Lost by 5 wickets

Date	Series	Match	Venue	Result
02 May 2004	England in West Indies 2003–04	West Indies v England	St Lucia	Lost by 5 wickets
05 May 2004	England in West Indies 2003–04	West Indies v England	Bridgetown	Won by 5 wickets

Series: England 2 West Indies 2

27 June 2004	NWB Series 2004	England v West Indies	Trent Bridge	Lost by 7 wickets
29 June 2004	NWB Series 2004	England v New Zealand	Riverside	Lost by 7 wickets
01 July 2004	NWB Series 2004	England v West Indies	Headingley	Won by 7 wickets
04 July 2004	NWB Series 2004	England v New Zealand	Bristol	Lost by 6 wickets
06 July 2004	NWB Series 2004	England v West Indies	Lord's	Lost by 7 wickets

Series: New Zealand beat West Indies in final

01 September 2004	NWB Challenge 2004	England v India	Trent Bridge	Won by 7 wickets
03 September 2004	NWB Challenge 2004	England v India	The Oval	Won by 70 runs
05 September 2004	NWB Challenge 2004	England v India	Lord's	Lost by 23 runs

Series: England 2 India 1

10 September 2004	ICC Trophy 2004	England v Zimbabwe	Edgbaston	Won by 152 runs
17 September 2004	ICC Trophy 2004	England v Sri Lanka	The Rose Bowl	Won by 49 runs
21 September 2004	ICC Trophy 2004	England v Australia	Edgbaston	Won by 6 wickets
25 September 2004	ICC Trophy 2004	England v West Indies	The Oval	Lost by 2 wickets

Series: West Indies beat England in final

28 November 2004	England in Zimbabwe 2004–05	Zimbabwe v England	Harare	Won by 5 wickets
01 December 2004	England in Zimbabwe 2004–05	Zimbabwe v England	Harare	Won by 161 runs
04 December 2004	England in Zimbabwe 2004–05	Zimbabwe v England	Bulawayo	Won by 8 wickets
05 December 2004	England in Zimbabwe 2004–05	Zimbabwe v England	Bulawayo	Won by 74 runs

Series: England 4 Zimbabwe 0

30 January 2005	England in South Africa 2004–05	South Africa v England	Johannesburg	Won by 26 runs
02 February 2005	England in South Africa 2004–05	South Africa v England	Bloemfontein	Match tied
06 February 2005	England in South Africa 2004–05	South Africa v England	Cape Town	Lost by 108 runs
09 February 2005	England in South Africa 2004–05	South Africa v England	East London	Lost by 7 wickets
11 February 2005	England in South Africa 2004–05	South Africa v England	Durban	No result
13 February 2005	England in South Africa 2004–05	South Africa v England	Centurion Park	Lost by 3 wickets

Series: England 1 South Africa 3

16 June 2005	NWB Series 2005	England v Bangladesh	The Oval	Won by 10 wickets
19 June 2005	NWB Series 2005	England v Australia	Bristol	Won by 3 wickets
21 June 2005	NWB Series 2005	England v Bangladesh	Trent Bridge	Won by 168 runs
28 June 2005	NWB Series 2005	England v Australia	Edgbaston	No result
02 July 2005	NWB Series 2005	England v Australia	Lord's	Match tied

Series: England and Australia tied

07 July 2005	NWB Challenge 2005	England v Australia	Headingley	Won by 9 wickets
10 July 2005	NWB Challenge 2005	England v Australia	Lord's	Lost by 7 wickets
12 July 2005	NWB Challenge 2005	England v Australia	The Oval	Lost by 8 wickets

Series: England 1 Australia 2

Michael Vaughan as Captain of England

	Inns	NO	Runs	HS	Avge	100	50	Overs	Mdns	Runs	Wkts	Avge	Best
Tests 31	58	5	1964	166	37.05	6	8	58	5	201	1	201.00	1/29
ODIs 48	46	9	1166	90*	31.51	–	10	62	0	320	4	80.00	2/42

THE ASHES 2005

Scorecards

THE ASHES 2005
First Test, Lord's, 21–24 July

Australia won by 239 runs

Australia won the toss
Umpires: Aleem Dar and RE Koertzen
Man of the Match: GD McGrath

Close of Play
Day 1: Australia 190, England 92/7 (Pietersen 28*)
Day 2: Australia 190 & 279/7 (Katich 10*); England 155
Day 3: Australia 190 & 384; England 155 & 156/5 (Pietersen 42*, GO Jones 6*)

Australia 1st innings			Runs	Mins	Balls	4s	6s
JL Langer	c Harmison	b Flintoff	40	77	44	5	–
ML Hayden		b Hoggard	12	38	25	2	–
*RT Ponting	c Strauss	b Harmison	9	38	18	1	–
DR Martyn	c GO Jones	b SP Jones	2	13	4	–	–
MJ Clarke	lbw	b SP Jones	11	35	22	2	–
SM Katich	c GO Jones	b Harmison	27	107	67	5	–
†AC Gilchrist	c GO Jones	b Flintoff	26	30	19	6	–
SK Warne		b Harmison	28	40	29	5	–
B Lee	c GO Jones	b Harmison	3	13	8	–	–
JN Gillespie	lbw	b Harmison	1	19	11	–	–
GD McGrath	not out		10	9	6	2	–
Extras	(b 5, lb 4, w 1, nb 11)		21				
TOTAL	(all out, 40.2 overs)		190				

FoW: 1–35, 2–55, 3–66, 4–66, 5–87, 6–126, 7–175, 8–178, 9–178, 10–190

Bowling	O	M	R	W	
Harmison	11.2	0	43	5	
Hoggard	8	0	40	1	(2nb)
Flintoff	11	2	50	2	(9nb)
SP Jones	10	0	48	2	(1w)

England 1st innings			Runs	Mins	Balls	4s	6s
ME Trescothick	c Langer	b McGrath	4	24	17	1	–
AJ Strauss	c Warne	b McGrath	2	28	21	–	–
*MP Vaughan		b McGrath	3	29	20	–	–
IR Bell		b McGrath	6	34	25	1	–
KP Pietersen	c Martyn	b Warne	57	148	89	8	2
A Flintoff		b McGrath	0	8	4	–	–
+GO Jones	c Gilchrist	b Lee	30	85	56	6	–
AF Giles	c Gilchrist	b Lee	11	14	13	2	–
MJ Hoggard	c Hayden	b Warne	0	18	16	–	–
SJ Harmison	c Martyn	b Lee	11	35	19	1	–
SP Jones	not out		20	21	14	3	–
Extras	(b 1, lb 5, nb 5)		11				
TOTAL	(all out, 48.1 overs)		155				

FoW: 1–10, 2–11, 3–18, 4–19, 5–21, 6–79, 7–92, 8–101, 9–122, 10–155

Bowling	O	M	R	W	
McGrath	18	5	53	5	
Lee	15.1	5	47	3	(4nb)
Gillespie	8	1	30	0	(1nb)
Warne	7	2	19	2	

Australia 2nd innings

			Runs	Mins	Balls	4s	6s
JL Langer	run out (Pietersen)		6	24	15	1	–
ML Hayden		b Flintoff	34	65	54	5	–
*RT Ponting	c sub	b Hoggard	42	100	65	3	–
DR Martyn	lbw	b Harmison	65	215	138	8	–
MJ Clarke		b Hoggard	91	151	106	15	–
SM Katich	c SP Jones	b Harmison	67	177	113	8	–
+AC Gilchrist		b Flintoff	10	26	14	1	–
SK Warne	c Giles	b Harmison	2	13	7	–	–
B Lee	run out (Giles)		8	16	16	1	–
JN Gillespie		b SP Jones	13	72	52	3	–
GD McGrath	not out		20	44	32	3	–
Extras	(b 10, lb 8, nb 8)		26				
TOTAL	(all out, 100.4 overs)		384				

FoW: 1–18, 2–54, 3–100, 4–255, 5–255, 6–274, 7–279, 8–289, 9–341, 10–384

Bowling	O	M	R	W	
Harmison	27.4	6	54	3	
Hoggard	16	1	56	2	(2nb)
Flintoff	27	4	123	2	(5nb)
SP Jones	18	1	69	1	(1nb)
Giles	11	1	56	0	
Bell	1	0	8	0	

England 2nd innings

			Runs	Mins	Balls	4s	6s
ME Trescothick	c Hayden	b Warne	44	128	103	8	0
AJ Strauss	c & b	Lee	37	115	67	6	0
*MP Vaughan		b Lee	4	47	26	1	0
IR Bell	lbw	b Warne	8	18	15	0	0
KP Pietersen	not out		64	120	79	6	2
A Flintoff	c Gilchrist	b Warne	3	14	11	0	0
+GO Jones	c Gillespie	b McGrath	6	51	27	1	0
AF Giles	c Hayden	b McGrath	0	2	2	0	0
MJ Hoggard	lbw	b McGrath	0	18	15	0	0
SJ Harmison	lbw	b Warne	0	3	1	0	0
SP Jones	c Warne	b McGrath	0	12	6	0	0
Extras	(b 6, lb 5, nb 3)		14				
TOTAL	(all out, 58.1 overs)		180				

FoW: 1–80, 2–96, 3–104, 4–112, 5–119, 6–158, 7–158, 8–164, 9–167, 10–180

Bowling	O	M	R	W	
McGrath	17.1	2	29	4	
Lee	15	3	58	2	(1nb)
Gillespie	6	0	18	0	(2nb)
Warne	20	2	64	4	

THE ASHES 2005
Second Test, Edgbaston, 4–7 August

England won by 2 runs

Australia won the toss
Umpires: BF Bowden and RE Koertzen
Man of the Match: A Flintoff

Close of Play
Day 1: England 407
Day 2: England 407 & 25/1 (Trescothick 19*, Hoggard 0*); Australia 308
Day 3: England 407 & 182; Australia 308 & 175/8 (Warne 20*)

England 1st innings			Runs	Mins	Balls	4s	6s
ME Trescothick	c Gilchrist	b Kasprowicz	90	143	102	15	2
AJ Strauss		b Warne	48	113	76	10	0
*MP Vaughan	c Lee	b Gillespie	24	54	41	3	0
IR Bell	c Gilchrist	b Kasprowicz	6	2	3	1	0
KP Pietersen	c Katich	b Lee	71	152	76	10	1
A Flintoff	c Gilchrist	b Gillespie	68	74	62	6	5
+GO Jones	c Gilchrist	b Kasprowicz	1	14	15	0	0
AF Giles	lbw	b Warne	23	34	30	4	0
MJ Hoggard	lbw	b Warne	16	62	49	2	0
SJ Harmison		b Warne	17	16	11	2	1
SP Jones	not out		19	39	24	1	1
Extras	(lb 9, w 1, nb 14)		24				
TOTAL	(all out, 79.2 overs)		407				

FoW: 1–112, 2–164, 3–170, 4–187, 5–290, 6–293, 7–342, 8–348, 9–375, 10–407

Bowling	O	M	R	W	
Lee	17	1	111	1	(3nb, 1w)
Gillespie	22	3	91	2	(3nb)
Kasprowicz	15	3	80	3	(8nb)
Warne	25.2	4	116	4	

Australia 1st innings			Runs	Mins	Balls	4s	6s
JL Langer	lbw	b SP Jones	82	276	154	7	0
ML Hayden	c Strauss	b Hoggard	0	5	1	0	0
*RT Ponting	c Vaughan	b Giles	61	87	76	12	0
DR Martyn	run out (Vaughan)		20	23	18	4	0
MJ Clarke	c GO Jones	b Giles	40	85	68	7	0
SM Katich	c GO Jones	b Flintoff	4	22	18	1	0
+AC Gilchrist	not out		49	120	69	4	0
SK Warne		b Giles	8	14	14	2	0
B Lee	c Flintoff	b SP Jones	6	14	10	1	0
JN Gillespie	lbw	b Flintoff	7	36	37	1	0
MS Kasprowicz	lbw	b Flintoff	0	1	1	0	0
Extras	(b 13, lb 7, w 1, nb 10)		31				
TOTAL	(all out, 76 overs)		308				

FoW: 1–0, 2–88, 3–118, 4–194, 5–208, 6–262, 7–273, 8–282, 9–308, 10–308

Bowling	O	M	R	W	
Harmison	11	1	48	0	(2nb)
Hoggard	8	0	41	1	(4nb)
SP Jones	16	2	69	2	(1nb, 1w)
Flintoff	15	1	52	3	(3nb)
Giles	26	2	78	3	

England 2nd innings

			Runs	Mins	Balls	4s	6s
ME Trescothick	c Gilchrist	b Lee	21	51	38	4	0
AJ Strauss		b Warne	6	28	12	1	0
MJ Hoggard	c Hayden	b Lee	1	35	27	0	0
*MP Vaughan		b Lee	1	2	2	0	0
IR Bell	c Gilchrist	b Warne	21	69	43	2	0
KP Pietersen	c Gilchrist	b Warne	20	50	35	0	2
A Flintoff		b Warne	73	133	86	6	4
+GO Jones	c Ponting	b Lee	9	33	19	1	0
AF Giles	c Hayden	b Warne	8	44	36	0	0
SJ Harmison	c Ponting	b Warne	0	2	1	0	0
SP Jones	not out		12	42	23	3	0
Extras	(lb 1, nb 9)		10				
TOTAL	(all out, 52.1 overs)		182				

FoW: 1–25, 2–27, 3–29, 4–31, 5–72, 6–75, 7–101, 8–131, 9–131, 10–182

Bowling	O	M	R	W	
Lee	18	1	82	4	(5nb)
Gillespie	8	0	24	0	(1nb)
Kasprowicz	3	0	29	0	(3nb)
Warne	23.1	7	46	6	

Australia 2nd innings

			Runs	Mins	Balls	4s	6s
JL Langer		b Flintoff	28	54	47	4	0
ML Hayden	c Trescothick	b SP Jones	31	106	64	4	0
*RT Ponting	c GO Jones	b Flintoff	0	4	5	0	0
DR Martyn	c Bell	b Hoggard	28	64	36	5	0
MJ Clarke		b Harmison	30	101	57	4	0
SM Katich	c Trescothick	b Giles	16	27	21	3	0
+AC Gilchrist	c Flintoff	b Giles	1	8	4	0	0
JN Gillespie	lbw	b Flintoff	0	4	2	0	0
SK Warne	hit wicket	b Flintoff	42	79	59	4	2
B Lee	not out		43	99	75	5	0
MS Kasprowicz	c GO Jones	b Harmison	20	60	31	3	0
Extras	(b 13, lb 8, w 1, nb 18)		40				
TOTAL	(all out, 64.3 overs)		279				

FoW: 1–47, 2–48, 3–82, 4–107, 5–134, 6–136, 7–137, 8–175, 9–220, 10–279

Bowling	O	M	R	W	
Harmison	17.3	3	62	2	(1nb, 1w)
Hoggard	5	0	26	1	
Giles	15	3	68	2	
Flintoff	22	3	79	4	(13nb)
SP Jones	5	1	23	1	

THE ASHES 2005
Third Test, Old Trafford, 11–15 August

Match drawn

England won the toss
Umpires: BF Bowden and SA Bucknor
Man of the Match: RT Ponting

Close of Play
Day 1: England 341/5 (Bell 59*)
Day 2: England 444; Australia 214/7 (Warne 45*, Gillespie 4*)
Day 3: England 444; Australia 264/7 (Warne 78*, Gillespie 7*)
Day 4: England 444 * 280/6dec; Australia 302 & 24/0 (Langer 14*, Hayden 5*)

England 1st innings			Runs	Mins	Balls	4s	6s
ME Trescothick	c Gilchrist	b Warne	63	196	117	9	0
AJ Strauss		b Lee	6	43	28	0	0
*MP Vaughan	c McGrath	b Katich	166	281	215	20	1
IR Bell	c Gilchrist	b Lee	59	205	155	8	0
KP Pietersen	c sub	b Lee	21	50	28	1	0
MJ Hoggard		b Lee	4	13	10	1	0
A Flintoff	c Langer	b Warne	46	93	67	7	0
+GO Jones		b Gillespie	42	86	51	6	0
AF Giles	c Hayden	b Warne	0	11	6	0	0
SJ Harmison	not out		10	13	11	1	0
SP Jones		b Warne	0	7	4	0	0
Extras	(b 4, lb 5, w 3, nb 15)		27				
TOTAL	(all out, 113.2 overs)		444				

FoW: 1–26, 2–163, 3–290, 4–333, 5–341, 6–346, 7–433, 8–434, 9–438, 10–444

Bowling	O	M	R	W	
McGrath	25	6	86	0	(4nb)
Lee	27	6	100	4	(5nb, 2w)
Gillespie	19	2	114	1	(2nb, 1w)
Warne	33.2	5	99	4	(2nb)
Katich	9	1	36	1	

Australia 1st innings			Runs	Mins	Balls	4s	6s
JL Langer	c Bell	b Giles	31	76	50	4	0
ML Hayden	lbw	b Giles	34	112	71	5	0
*RT Ponting	c Bell	b SP Jones	7	20	12	1	0
DR Martyn		b Giles	20	71	41	2	0
SM Katich		b Flintoff	17	39	28	1	0
+AC Gilchrist	c GO Jones	b SP Jones	30	74	49	4	0
SK Warne	c Giles	b SP Jones	90	183	122	11	1
MJ Clarke	c Flintoff	b SP Jones	7	19	18	0	0
JN Gillespie	lbw	b SP Jones	26	144	111	1	1
B Lee	c Trescothick	b SP Jones	1	17	16	0	0
GD McGrath	not out		1	20	4	0	0
Extras	(b 8, lb 7, w 8, nb 15)		38				
TOTAL	(all out, 84.5 overs)		302				

FoW: 1–58, 2–73, 3–86, 4–119, 5–133, 6–186, 7–201, 8–287, 9–293, 10–302

Bowling	O	M	R	W	
Harmison	10	0	47	0	(3nb)
Hoggard	6	2	22	0	
Flintoff	20	1	65	1	(8nb)
SP Jones	17.5	6	53	6	(1nb, 2w)
Giles	31	4	100	3	(1w)

England 2nd innings

			Runs	Mins	Balls	4s	6s
ME Trescothick		b McGrath	41	71	56	6	0
AJ Strauss	c Martyn	b McGrath	106	246	158	9	2
*MP Vaughan	c sub	b Lee	14	45	37	2	0
IR Bell	c Katich	b McGrath	65	165	103	4	1
KP Pietersen	lbw	b McGrath	0	3	1	0	0
A Flintoff		b McGrath	4	20	18	0	0
+GO Jones	not out		27	15	12	2	2
AF Giles	not out		0	4	0	0	0
Extras	(b 5, lb 3, w 1, nb 14)		23				
TOTAL	(6 wickets dec, 61.5 overs)		280				

DNB: MJ Hoggard, SJ Harmison, SP Jones

FoW: 1–64, 2–97, 3–224, 4–225, 5–248, 6–264

Bowling	O	M	R	W	
McGrath	20.5	1	115	5	(6nb, 1w)
Lee	12	0	60	1	(4nb)
Warne	25	3	74	0	
Gillespie	4	0	23	0	(4nb)

Australia 2nd innings

			Runs	Mins	Balls	4s	6s
JL Langer	c GO Jones	b Hoggard	14	42	41	3	0
ML Hayden		b Flintoff	36	123	91	5	1
*RT Ponting	c GO Jones	b Harmison	156	411	275	16	1
DR Martyn	lbw	b Harmison	19	53	36	3	0
SM Katich	c Giles	b Flintoff	12	30	23	2	0
+AC Gilchrist	c Bell	b Flintoff	4	36	30	0	0
MJ Clarke		b SP Jones	39	73	63	7	0
JN Gillespie	lbw	b Hoggard	0	8	5	0	0
SK Warne	c GO Jones	b Flintoff	34	99	69	5	0
B Lee	not out		18	44	25	4	0
GD McGrath	not out		5	17	9	1	0
Extras	(b 5, lb 8, w 1, nb 20)		34				
TOTAL	(9 wickets, 108 overs)		371				

FoW: 1–25, 2–96, 3–129, 4–165, 5–182, 6–263, 7–264, 8–340, 9–354

Bowling	O	M	R	W	
Harmison	22	4	67	2	(4nb, 1w)
Hoggard	13	0	49	2	(6nb)
Giles	26	4	93	0	
Vaughan	5	0	21	0	
Flintoff	25	6	71	4	(9nb)
SP Jones	17	3	57	1	

THE ASHES 2005
Fourth Test, Trent Bridge, 25–28 August

England won by 3 wickets

England won the toss
Umpires: Aleem Dar and SA Bucknor
Man of the Match: A Flintoff

Close of Play
Day 1: England 229/4 (Pietersen 33*, Flintoff 8*)
Day 2: England 477; Australia 99/5 (Katich 20*)
Day 3: England 477; Australia 218 & 222/4 (Clarke 39*, Katich 24*)

England 1st innings			Runs	Mins	Balls	4s	6s
ME Trescothick		b Tait	65	138	111	8	1
AJ Strauss	c Hayden	b Warne	35	99	64	4	0
*MP Vaughan	c Gilchrist	b Ponting	58	138	99	9	0
IR Bell	c Gilchrist	b Tait	3	12	5	0	0
KP Pietersen	c Gilchrist	b Lee	45	131	108	6	0
A Flintoff	lbw	b Tait	102	201	132	14	1
+GO Jones	c &	b Kasprowicz	85	205	149	8	0
AF Giles	lbw	b Warne	15	45	35	3	0
MJ Hoggard	c Gilchrist	b Warne	10	46	28	1	0
SJ Harmison	st Gilchrist	b Warne	2	9	6	0	0
SP Jones	not out		15	32	27	3	0
Extras	(b 1, lb 15, w 1, nb 25)		42				
TOTAL	(all out, 123.1 overs)		477				

FoW: 1–105, 2–137, 3–146, 4–213, 5–241, 6–418, 7–450, 8–450, 9–454, 10–477

Bowling	O	M	R	W	
Lee	32	2	131	1	(8nb)
Kasprowicz	32	3	122	1	(13nb)
Tait	24	4	97	3	(4nb)
Warne	29.1	4	102	4	
Ponting	6	2	9	1	(1w)

Australia 1st innings			Runs	Mins	Balls	4s	6s
JL Langer	c Bell	b Hoggard	27	95	59	5	0
ML Hayden	lbw	b Hoggard	7	41	27	1	0
*RT Ponting	lbw	b SP Jones	1	6	6	0	0
DR Martyn	lbw	b Hoggard	1	4	3	0	0
MJ Clarke	lbw	b Harmison	36	93	53	5	0
SM Katich	c Strauss	b SP Jones	45	91	66	7	0
+AC Gilchrist	c Strauss	b Flintoff	27	58	36	3	1
SK Warne	c Bell	b SP Jones	0	2	1	0	0
B Lee	c Bell	b SP Jones	47	51	44	5	3
MS Kasprowicz		b SP Jones	5	8	7	1	0
SW Tait	not out		3	27	9	0	0
Extras	(lb 2, w 1, nb 16)		19				
TOTAL	(all out, 49.1 overs)		218				

FoW: 1–20, 2–21, 3–22, 4–58, 5–99, 6–157, 7–157, 8–163, 9–175, 10–218

Bowling	O	M	R	W	
Harmison	9	1	48	1	(3nb)
Hoggard	15	3	70	3	(4nb)
SP Jones	14.1	4	44	5	(1nb)
Flintoff	11	1	54	1	(8nb, 1w)

Australia 2nd innings

			Runs	Mins	Balls	4s	6s
JL Langer	c Bell	b Giles	61	149	112	8	0
ML Hayden	c Giles	b Flintoff	26	57	41	4	0
*RT Ponting	run out (sub GJ Pratt)		48	137	89	3	1
DR Martyn	c GO Jones	b Flintoff	13	56	30	1	0
MJ Clarke	c GO Jones	b Hoggard	56	209	170	6	0
SM Katich	lbw	b Harmison	59	262	183	4	0
+AC Gilchrist	lbw	b Hoggard	11	20	11	2	0
SK Warne	st GO Jones	b Giles	45	68	42	5	2
B Lee	not out		26	77	39	3	0
MS Kasprowicz	c GO Jones	b Harmison	19	30	26	1	0
SW Tait		b Harmison	4	20	16	1	0
Extras	(b 1, lb 4, nb 14)		19				
TOTAL	(all out, 124 overs)		387				

FoW: 1–50, 2–129, 3–155, 4–161, 5–261, 6–277, 7–314, 8–342, 9–373, 10–387

Bowling	O	M	R	W	
Hoggard	27	7	72	2	(1nb)
SP Jones	4	0	15	0	
Harmison	30	5	93	3	(1nb)
Flintoff	29	4	83	2	(9nb)
Giles	28	3	107	2	
Bell	6	2	12	0	(3nb)

England 2nd innings

			Runs	Mins	Balls	4s	6s
ME Trescothick	c Ponting	b Warne	27	24	22	4	0
AJ Strauss	c Clarke	b Warne	23	68	37	3	0
*MP Vaughan	c Hayden	b Warne	0	8	6	0	0
IR Bell	c Kasprowicz	b Lee	3	38	20	0	0
KP Pietersen	c Gilchrist	b Lee	23	51	34	3	0
A Flintoff		b Lee	26	63	34	3	0
+GO Jones	c Kasprowicz	b Warne	3	25	13	0	0
AF Giles	not out		7	30	17	0	0
MJ Hoggard	not out		8	20	13	1	0
Extras	(lb 4, nb 5)		9				
TOTAL	(7 wickets, 31.5 overs)		129				

DNB: SJ Harmison, SP Jones

FoW: 1–32, 2–36, 3–57, 4–57, 5–103, 6–111, 7–116

Bowling	O	M	R	W	
Lee	12	0	51	3	(5nb)
Kasprowicz	2	0	19	0	
Warne	13.5	2	31	4	
Tait	4	0	24	0	

THE ASHES 2005
Fifth Test, The Oval, 8–12 September

Match drawn

England won the toss
Umpires: B.F.Bowden and R.E.Koertzen
Man of the Match: KP Pietersen
Men of the Series: A Flintoff/SK Warne

Close of Play
Day 1: England 319/7 (Jones 21*, Giles 5*; 88 overs)
Day 2: England 373, Australia 112/0 (Langer 75*, Hayden 32*; 33 overs)
Day 3: Australia 277/2 (Hayden 110*, Martyn 9*; 78.4 overs)
Day 4: Australia 367, England 34/1 (Trescothick 14*, Vaughan 19*; 13.2 overs)

England 1st innings			Runs	Mins	Balls	4s	6s
ME Trescothick	c Hayden	b Warne	43	77	65	8	0
AJ Strauss	c Katich	b Warne	129	351	210	17	0
*MP Vaughan	c Clarke	b Warne	11	26	25	2	0
IR Bell	lbw	b Warne	0	9	7	0	0
KP Pietersen		b Warne	14	30	25	2	0
A Flintoff	c Warne	b McGrath	72	162	115	12	1
PD Collingwood	lbw	b Tait	7	26	26	1	0
+GO Jones		b Lee	25	60	41	5	0
AF Giles	lbw	b Warne	32	120	70	1	0
MJ Hoggard	c Martyn	b McGrath	2	47	36	0	0
SJ Harmison	not out		20	25	20	4	0
Extras	(b 4, lb 6, w 1, nb 7)		18				
TOTAL	(all out, 105.3 overs)		373				

FoW: 1–82, 2–102, 3–104, 4–131, 5–274, 6–289), 7–297, 8–325, 9–345, 10–373

Bowling	O	M	R	W	
McGrath	27	5	72	2	(1w)
Lee	23	3	94	1	(3nb)
Tait	15	1	61	1	(3nb)
Warne	37.3	5	122	6	
Katich	3	0	14	0	

Australia 1st innings			Runs	Mins	Balls	4s	6s
JL Langer		b Harmison	105	233	146	11	2
ML Hayden	lbw	b Flintoff	138	416	303	18	–
*RT Ponting	c Strauss	b Flintoff	35	81	56	3	–
DR Martyn	c Collingwood	b Flintoff	10	36	29	1	–
MJ Clarke	lbw	b Hoggard	25	119	59	2	–
SM Katich	lbw	b Flintoff	1	12	11	–	–
+AC Gilchrist	lbw	b Hoggard	23	32	20	4	–
SK Warne	c Vaughan	b Flintoff	0	18	10	–	–
B Lee	c Giles	b Hoggard	6	22	10	–	–
GD McGrath	c Strauss	b Hoggard	0	6	6	–	–
SW Tait	not out		1	7	2	–	–
Extras	(b 4, lb 8, w 2, nb 9)		23				
TOTAL	(all out, 107.1 overs)		367				

FoW: 1–185, 2–264, 3–281, 4–323, 5–329. 6–356, 7–359, 8–363, 9–363, 10–367

Bowling	O	M	R	W	
Harmison	22	2	87	1	(2nb, 2w)
Hoggard	24.1	2	97	4	(1nb)
Flintoff	34	10	78	5	(6nb)
Giles	23	1	76	0	
Collingwood	4	0	17	0	

England 2nd innings			Runs	Mins	Balls	4s	6s
ME Trescothick	lbw	b Warne	33	150	84	1	–
AJ Strauss	c Katich	b Warne	1	16	7	–	–
*MP Vaughan	c Gilchrist	b McGrath	45	80	65	6	–
IR Bell	c Warne	b McGrath	0	2	1	–	–
KP Pietersen		b McGrath	158	283	187	15	7
A Flintoff	c &	b Warne	8	20	13	1	–
PD Collingwood	c Ponting	b Warne	10	70	51	1	–
+GO Jones		b Tait	1	22	12	–	–
AF Giles		b Warne	59	158	97	7	–
MJ Hoggard	not out		4	44	35	–	–
SJ Harmison	c Hayden	b Warne	0	1	2	–	–
Extras	(b 4, w 7, nb 5)		16				
TOTAL	(all out, 91.3 overs)		335				

FoW: 1–2, 2–67, 3–67, 4–109, 5–126, 6–186, 7–199, 8–308, 9–335, 10–335

Bowling	O	M	R	W	
McGrath	26	3	85	3	(1nb)
Lee	20	4	88	0	(4nb, 1w)
Warne	38.3	3	124	6	(1w)
Clarke	2	0	6	0	
Tait	5	0	28	1	(1w)

Australia 2nd innings		Runs	Mins	Balls	4s	6s
JL Langer	not out	0	2	4	–	–
ML Hayden	not out	0	2	–	–	–
Extras		0				
TOTAL	(for 0 wickets, 0.4 overs)	0				

DNB: *RT Ponting, DR Martyn, MJ Clarke, SM Katich, +AC Gilchrist, SK Warne, B Lee, GD McGrath, SW Tait

Bowling	O	M	R	W
Harmison	0.4	0	0	0

INDEX